Antonio Cardinal Bacci

Antonio Cardinal Bacci

Essays in Appreciation of His Life, His Latinity, and His Books

ON THE FIFTIETH ANNIVERSARY
OF HIS DEATH (1971–2021)

Edited by
PIER CARLO TAGLIAFERRI

with a letter of introduction from
ARCHBISHOP LORIS FRANCESCO CAPOVILLA

Translated and with a Foreword by
ANTHONY LO BELLO

AROUCA PRESS

Originally published as *Il Cardinale Antonio Bacci*
by Pagnini Editore (Florence), 2005
Kind permission granted for this English translation.

Copyright © Arouca Press 2021
English translation & Foreword © Anthony Lo Bello 2021

All rights reserved:
No part of this book may be reproduced or transmitted,
in any form or by any means, without permission

ISBN: 978-1-98990-583-8 (pbk)
ISBN: 978-1-98990-584-5 (hc)

Arouca Press
PO Box 55003
Bridgeport PO
Waterloo, ON N2J 3G0
Canada
www.aroucapress.com
Send inquiries to info@aroucapress.com

CONTENTS

Foreword of the Translator. ix
Introduction of Paolo Ruffini liii
From the Editor lv
Letter of Msgr. Loris Francesco Capovilla
   to the editor. lvii

1 Antonio Cardinal Bacci: Biographical Notes
    Nello Lascialfari 1
2 The Latinity of Antonio Cardinal Bacci
    Carlo Nardi. 9
3 The Works of Antonio Cardinal Bacci
    Pier Carlo Tagliaferri 21

   Bibliography 61
   Illustrations. 63
   Index 75
   About the Translator 81

FOREWORD

THE NAME OF ANTONIO BACCI WILL NEVER be forgotten by those who love what he called *the Catholic language*. He put his learning to use in the service of the Popes, whose Latin expert he was for three decades. All the Papal encyclicals that were issued in Latin during the period 1931 to 1960 were written under his supervision. In skill of Latin composition he had no rival. Among the most learned cardinals of the last century, he must be numbered with Giovanni Mercati (1866–1957) and Eugène Tisserant (1884–1972). For a brief autobiographical account of his own life up to 1964, see Bacci's memoirs *With Latin in the Service of the Popes*, published by Arouca Press in 2020.

The present volume is the translation of a small book published in memory of Cardinal Bacci by the Archives of the Archdiocese of Florence in cooperation with the *Banca del Mugello Credito Cooperativo*, a bank in the Mugello region of Tuscany that had its origins in a savings and loan association that Antonio Bacci helped found as a young priest. There are three contributors to the volume:

Msgr. Nello Lascialfari (1923–2021) was secretary to four cardinal-archbishops of Florence, Giovanni Benelli (1921–1982, archbishop of Florence 1977–1982), Silvano Piovanelli (1924–2016, archbishop of Florence 1983–2001), Ennio Antonelli (1936–2008, archbishop of Florence 2001–2008), and Giuseppe Betori (b. 1947, current archbishop of Florence since 2008).

Carlo Nardi (b. 1951) is Professor of Patristics on the Faculty of Theology of the University of Central Italy (Florence).

Pier Carlo Tagliaferri (b. 1938) is a professor, author and editor, particularly prolific in matters of local Tuscan interest.

The preliminary matter by Paolo Ruffini, Pier Carlo Tagliaferri, and Archbishop Capovilla, as well as Tagliaferri's contribution entitled *The Works of Antonio Cardinal Bacci*, were written especially for this volume. The latter essay is missing a discussion of Bacci's *Meditazioni per tutti i giorni dell'anno*,[1] but the English translation of that work, *Meditations for Each Day* (1965), was recently republished by Arouca Press in 2018, so the reader may easily satisfy his curiosity in this regard. The essays by Nello Lascialfari and Carlo Nardi had previously appeared in a *Festschrift* celebrating the twentieth anniversary of the elevation of Silvano Piovanelli, formerly Archbishop of Florence, to the cardinalate.[2] Bacci's foreword to the controversial volume of Tito Casini is reproduced without discussion in Lascialfari's essay; this is to be expected since Bacci had a low opinion of the liturgical renewal of the sixties, an enterprise which he believed ruined the liturgy and removed a protective fence from around the Catholic faith. Such an attitude is awkward to consider for the authors of officially approved publications. For the same reason, no doubt, there is also no discussion of Bacci's cosigning in 1969, together with Alfredo Cardinal Ottaviani, of a protest against the revision of the Missal.

Quite fortunate was the inclusion of several examples of Bacci's Italian poems in the contribution of Tagliaferri. Certainly the reader will not ascribe to Bacci the faults of my own inadequate translations of those pieces.

However, the lasting contribution of Antonio Bacci is his scientific work for the promotion of the Latin language in the twentieth century, and it is therefore to this topic that my *Foreword*, and this whole volume as well, is primarily devoted. In the pages that follow the reader will find translations of passages from Bacci's writings on this subject not heretofore available in English. I will also not fail to notice the continuation of his scientific work undertaken by his colleagues and successors after his death.

Bacci's intellectual activity served to promote Latin in

---

1   Turin, Marietti, 1959, 944 pages.
2   Collana: Pubblicazioni dell'Archivio arcivescovile di Firenze, Studi e testi 9, *Firenze e i suoi cardinali, Studi offerti al card. Silvano Piovanelli del titolo di Santa Maria delle Grazie a Via Trionfale, arcivescovo emerito di Firenze in occasione del XX anniversario dell'elevazione alla dignità cardinalizia, 1985, 25 Maggio–2005*, Firenze, Pagnini, 2005, 131-139.

Foreword

two different but related respects, as the official language of the Catholic Church and as a contemporary means of communication among learned men who do not speak the same native language. Since his death the position of Latin has, alas, collapsed on both fronts. In the secular world, the study of Latin in colleges and universities began to decline as those places became less populated by gentlemen and less staffed by instructors in holy orders. The rise of the sciences and the development of good literature in the several modern languages resulted in Latin no longer being seen by the commonality of educators as necessary for a liberal education. It thereupon ceased to be a required subject in the schools; as a result it is no longer offered in most high schools, and the percentage of professors at an American liberal arts college or university who can translate a sentence of Latin unseen is about 1%, down from 100% a century and a half ago. The education offered in these establishments today is entirely vocational since the majority of their students have no interest in studying good literature for its own sake in any language but see a college education as a means of gaining employment; higher education is now a big business and so it answers to the demands of its customers. Latin formerly was the language of international corrrspondence between governments; thus, for example, Oliver Cromwell employed John Milton as his Latin secretary to communicate with other sovereigns and their ministers. When George I consulted with his Prime Minister Robert Walpole, they conversed in Latin, the only language they had in common. By the eighteenth century French began to replace Latin for this diplomatic purpose, and its hold was firm until English rose into prominence in the twentieth century. If scholars or diplomats from different countries meet who would formerly have conversed in Latin, they are now likely to communicate in English or to remain helpless in frustrating and awkward silence. Conditions in the secular world encouraged elements in the Catholic Church who saw value in the demands of the sixteenth century reformers that the language of the liturgy be vernacular. The result was that the attitude that prevailed in the outside world became dominant in the Church as well. Bacci was modern enough not to want Latin for everybody. He believed that Latin should be the common language of the learned of the world, not the language of paperboys and milkmaids. Unlike French or English, Latin did not require implicit recognition from the part of anyone that the language of another country, perhaps a foe or a rival, was preeminent. In the case of the Church, Bacci saw the fall of Latin as a catastrophe that would level the liturgy to the ground and cause the *una sancta catholica et apostolica ecclesia* to disintegrate into chaos and lose all continuity with its past history.

Antonio Bacci was born during the reign of Leo XIII, the greatest Latinist on the papal throne since Pius II and the author of odes in the style of Horace. By the time he died, Bacci had witnessed the abolition of his own office and the removal of Latin from the liturgy. The steady decline of Latin at the Holy See has only accelerated in the past decade, and the current situation is one that would have horrified the Popes for whom Bacci wrote. How did this happen?

The chief Latinists at the Holy See were the Secretary of Briefs to Princes (*ab Epistulis Summi Pontificis ad Principes, Segretario dei Brevi ai Principi*) and the Secretary for Latin Letters (*ab Epistulis latinis Summi Pontificis, Segretario delle Lettere Latine Pontificie*). The former official conducted the most important correspondence and composed the major Papal documents. He came forward into the spotlight every now and then when he presented the *Oratio de eligendo pontifice*, which it was his duty to compose and deliver before the cardinals assembled for the Papal conclave. After having discharged these responsibilities for a certain period of time, he might expect to receive the red hat. The Secretary for Latin Letters was the functionary next in rank who wrote the less important items. He was, though, the usual fellow called upon to deliver the eulogy at the funeral of a Pope. The last Secretary of Briefs

Foreword

to Princes was Amleto Tondini (1899-1969), the successor of Cardinal Bacci. In the period 1950-1954 Tondini had been the top man, the *Reggente*, at the Apostolic Chancery, for it took Pius XII twelve years to fill the vacancy in the office of Chancellor of the Holy Roman Church caused by the death of Tommaso Pio Cardinal Boggiani in 1942[3]; in his capacity as *Reggente* he wrote the *biglietti* or letters of appointment to the College of Cardinals and to bishoprics. The last of the Secretaries for Latin Letters was the Istrian Giuseppe Del Ton (1900-1997). Pope Paul VI abolished both positions in 1967. The Latinists thereafter constituted the Latin Letters Office of the Secretariat of State. Their work load was increased when Pope Paul abolished the Apostolic Chancery in 1973, for thereafter they had to write the *biglietti* of appointment as well. In the period 1970-2009, an American had the highest visibility of the experts in this Office. This was Reginald Foster (1939-2020), who first came to Antonio Bacci's notice when as a student in an American Carmelite seminary he submitted his Latin translation of the Gettysburg Address for the future cardinal's inspection. Bacci replied and advised him to improve his style by studying the best authors. This reminded me of the advice of Basil Lanneau Gildersleeve (1831-1924) to a student who wanted to learn Greek; the boy was advised to read nothing but Greek for five years. Many years later Foster visited Bacci, by that time retired, in his office in the Vatican; this suite of rooms would in due course become Foster's own, for after the death of Tondini, Foster was brought into the Latin Letters Office at the recommendation of his teacher Karl Egger, whose lectures Foster had been attending in Rome at the "empty, dying and now truly dead" Institute of Higher Latin at the Salesian Pontifical University.[4]

Bacci's masterpiece is his *Vocabolario italiano-latino delle parole moderne e difficili a tradurre*, which went through four

---

3 He eventually appointed Celso Cardinal Costantini (1876-1958).
4 The words are Foster's. He was speaking in 2017 of the situation in May, 1970.

editions (1944, 1949, 1955, 1963). It was originally published as the second part of a volume entitled *Varia latinitatis scripta*, the first part of which, called *Inscriptiones, Orationes, Epistulae*, was a selection from Bacci's compositions illustrating the use of Latin in modern situations. The first edition contained the following preface:

> Not a few people in the Roman Curia have asked me, and that more than once, how to translate into Latin many words that are not found in the usual dictionaries or are translated there inaccurately. It is at their bidding to do something to the best of my abilities that I have published this lexicon, which in fact I had already written long ago at the request of a student. This work is certainly neither perfect nor complete, all the labor and study that I devoted to it notwithstanding.
>
> It seemed good to include at the beginning of this book some examples of my Latin compositions that had already been published or that were in the process of being revised and polished. This is certainly a small thing, but since Latin letters are almost everywhere silent, my humble attempts in this genre seemed—unless I am mistaken—perhaps to have some value.
>
> As regards the dictionary portion, I ask, dear reader, that if you should come upon anything missing or needing correction, please do me the courtesy of bringing it to my attention. For if at some time in the future God, men, and the publishers decide on a second edition, I would like it to be a corrected and enlarged one. Hail and farewell!

Bacci sent a copy of the book to Pius XII and a second copy to Giovanni Battista Montini at the Secretariat of State. He received the following letter of acknowledgment:

> The August Pontiff has gratefully and gladly accepted, and not only on his own behalf, the volume *Varia latinitatis scripta* which you sent Him as a gift. Your book offers the Most Blessed Father the perfect opportunity

Foreword

publicly to commend you for your unique knowledge of Latin literature, for which He has personally on more than one occasion congratulated you face-to-face when in your official capacity you presented Him with compositions worthy of all praise and abundantly adorned not less by their richness and variety of learning than by their polished elegance of expression and flower of speech.

The Common Father of all furthermore rejoices that you have published a book that will be as useful as imaginable to lovers of the Latin language because you, after the most productive study and work, transmit therein translations and word equivalents not only chosen from the best Roman authors but also "prudently" invented in accordance with the genius of the ancients, whereby the more difficult words and phrases from modern languages may be expressed in Latin. Furthermore, by means of the numerous examples of compositions in every branch of authorship which you offer, you truly pave the road so to speak towards an appreciation of the beauties of Latin.

Would that a great number of the clergy, especially those working in the Roman Curia, might be motivated by this excellent work of literature to a more diligent use of the Latin language, so that that high regard for liberal studies that in former times flourished under the patronage of the Supreme Pontiffs might not cease to thrive in these our own times.

Wherefore the August Pontiff, expressing His grateful appreciation for the testimony of your respect communicated to Him, with the utmost paternal goodwill imparts to you His Apostolic Benediction, the assurance of every divine favor.

I take this opportunity to declare my own special regard for you and most willingly sign myself

Very respectfully yours,
J. B. Montini

When demand called for a third edition, it was decided to separate the two parts of *Varia latinitatis scripta* and publish each as a separate volume, the dictionary under the title *Lexicon eorum vocabulorum quae difficilius latine redduntur (Vocabolario italiano-latino delle parole moderne e difficili a tradurre)*, and the chrestomathy as *Inscriptiones Orationes Epistulae*.

One problem that complicates and no doubt limits the use of Bacci's *Lexicon* is the fact that it is Italian-Latin. If, for example, one wants to know how to say *privy chamberlain* in Latin, one has to know first how to say it in Italian, *cameriere segreto*; one can then look up the latter phrase in Bacci's *Lexicon*. For this problem there is no solution. One characteristic of the *Lexicon* that is immediately obvious is that Bacci is a *Ciceronian*, that is, he looks to the usage of the *classical* period of the Golden Age of Latin letters, the era of Julius Caesar, Cicero, Horace, Livy, Ovid, Vergil, and the few decades thereafter as determinative of what is Latin of the highest quality. In this he is surely right, since if one wants to learn how to write well in any language, one can only do so by recourse to the best authors, the *probati scriptores*, of that language. The problem this fact presents for Bacci's enterprise is that the vocabulary of Christianity developed in the centuries that followed this Golden Age. The period of approximately two centuries immediately following this Classical Age, Bacci calls the *tempora serioris Latinitatis*, that is, the era of *Late Latin*. The following era embracing the third through the sixth centuries he denominates the *tempora cadentis Latinitatis*, or the age of Latin in decline. This age includes the authors Arnobius, Augustine, Caelius Aurelianus, Diomedes, Jerome, Lactantius, Lucius Appuleius, Marcellus Empiricus, Priscianus, Prudentius, Sextus Aurelius Victor, and Tertullian. Examples of words that he assigns to the period of Late Latin are *filialis, graecitas, incorruptibilitas, inscrutabilis, insensibilis, rotabilis, sanctificator, sollemnitas,* and *visibilis*. Examples of words he marks as of the period of *cadentis Latinitatis* are *impaenitens, impaenitentia, impassibilis, incorruptilis, oblatio, passibilis, sanctificare, scrutinium,* and *venialis*. Following the period of Late Latin there came the age of *Low*

Foreword

Latin, called by Bacci *infima Latinitas*. In this period Latin became heavily ecclesiastical. Belonging to this time are such words as *cancellaria, dataria, indefectibilis, indulgentia, inspiratio, missa,* and *secretarius* and the phrases *a secretis status, indulgentia plenaria,* and *indulgentia partialis.* Bacci does not propose to touch these words when they occur in the liturgy, but he does not recommend their use in modern composition. He always maintained that there was a difference between writing Latin and writing ecclesiastically.[5] Writing "Church Latin" usually involves taking over words directly from the vernacular languages in the same manner as that of a friend of mine who, writing to tell me that a colleague U. R. had died while jogging, wrote, "*U. R. mortuus est joggans per agros.*" Examples of "ecclesiastical" words followed by their equivalents in Ciceronian Latin suggested by Bacci are:

bonus latinus =	Latinitas
canonicatus =	canonici munus
cardinalatus =	Patrum Cardinalium munus
canonizare =	in Sanctorum numerum referre
capella =	sacellum
civilitas =	civilis cultus
classici =	scriptores optimi
compassio =	commiseratio
confraternitas =	sodalitas
conscientiam examinare =	animi latrebras scrutari
devotio =	pietas
dispensare aliquem a lege =	aliquem lege exsolvere
generalatus =	summi moderatoris munus
optimus latinus =	optimum latine scribendi genus
Papa =	Pontifex Maximus
praedicator =	contionator
provincialatus =	provinciae moderandae munus
respectus =	observantia
Salvator =	Servator

---

5 *Quid sit ecclesiastice scribere et quid latine*, in *Latinitas*, volume 1, number 2, April, 1953, pages 90-95.

Bacci's three-column entry *Salvatore* was perhaps the most famous in the *Lexicon*; in it he proposes as the best Latin equivalent the noun *Servator* to be found in Cicero and explains why he does not say *Salvator*. In this strategy Bacci relied on the infallible support of the greatest of Italian philologists Egidio Forcellini (1688-1768) and of Pope Leo XIII (1810-1903) and his Latin secretary Alessandro Volpini (1844-1903). In the entry *Messa* (i. e. *Mass*) Bacci gives the translation *Sacrum -i, n.* Thus, people who had gotten into the habit of writing ecclesiastical Latin were in for a shock. In the following decades, the Latin secretaries, at the insistence of less learned superior prelates, were forced to abandon the use of perfectly good Ciceronian words such as *usurpo, usurpare* (to use) and *concupio, concupire* (to desire earnestly) because the higher authorities feared that using them would conjure up in the minds of readers the modern cognate derivative words, in these two cases *usurp* and *concupiscence*, which had problematic meanings not present in the original Latin verbs.

Not a few of the readers of Bacci's *Lexicon* remarked on his policy with regard to the use of *i, I, j, J, u, U,* and *v, V*. The fourth and last edition of Bacci's Lexicon (1963) contained an instructive *Introduction* which dealt with this and other matters I have mentioned above:

> I. Although the list of words proposed for Latin translation in this *Lexicon* are Italian, the entries themselves are written in Latin, with only occasional necessary translations and comments in the various modern languages. This is not only in order that this dictionary may be serviceable to those of other nations who do not understand Italian, but also that it may conform in a certain way to the plan according to which the lexicons of Forcellini and Morcelli were composed.
>
> In this respect it must be observed that in former times Latin dictionaries, grammars, and other such instructional aids, if intended for those who had already learned the elements of the language, were written themselves in Latin so that students,

Foreword

by necessity and with an example of the very goal of their efforts set before their eyes, might more easily be attracted and encouraged to learn, write, and speak the most noble language of the Romans.

For this reason I found myself inclined to follow the same path and tread in the same footsteps as those lexicographers.

II. Approximately two thousand new words have been added in this fourth, corrected edition.

III. In the Latin language there is no capital *U* or small case *v*, only *V* and *u*. These letters, although written differently, are nevertheless pronounced similarly, although this sound is sometimes that of a vowel (for example, *VBI* = *ubi*) and sometimes that of a consonant or rather semi-consonant, that is, in that bilabial way that the English pronounce *Westminster*. Never does the Latin letter have the sound of the letter *v* as pronounced by the modern Italians and other peoples; this labiodental sound was completely unknown to the Latin speakers of old. Thus, one writes in Latin *Vltimus*, *Volo*, and *uulgus*, *seruus*, *uita*, and *uiuere* and likewise for all other words with the letter *V-u*.

Similarly the letter *i* is usually a vowel but sometimes a consonant or a semi-consonant.

That the two letters *V-u* and *i* now and then have the force of a consonant is clearly established by the following passages from Quintilian:

"A grammarian may ask, 'Why is it that two and only two vowels, *i* and *u*, can be doubled in the same syllable, although no consonant can? For example, in *coniicit*, which comes from *cum* and *iacit*, *i* follows *i*, and in *uulgus* and *seruus*, *u* follows *u*.' We answer that Cicero wrote *aiio* and *Maiiam* with double *i*, and when he did this the first *i* was pronounced like a consonant."[6]

"...and even in the case of those two vowels, the grammarian must determine whether sometimes

---

6 Quint. I, 11. Cf. G. B. Pighi, *Questioni di ortografia: I. La doppia i intervocalica*. Extract from *Rendiconto delle Sessioni dell'Accademia delle Scienze dell'Istituto di Bologna*, series V, vol. V, 1953, page 1 and following.

they are effectively consonants, because the *i* in *iam* is written like that in *etiam*, and the *u* in *uos* like that in *tuos*."7

Priscianus furthermore confidently asserts that the letter *i*, when it occurs between two vowels, even if it is not doubled, is still treated and pronounced as if it were doubled, and the three words that follow must be divided into syllables thus: *pei-ius, mai-ius, ei-ius*, etc.8

Now since the letters *V-u*, and *i* do not always have the same sound, but sometimes act as vowels and sometimes as consonants, it so happened that in the course of time two forms of the same letter wisely came into use, namely *i-j (I-J)* and *u-v (U-V)*. But this only occurred after Latin had become the language solely of the learned class, who thereby distinguished for readers and writers that double pronunciation of which both I and Quintilian have spoken above.

Thus in the most ancient manuscripts one never finds *J-j*, nor does *u* differ from the letter *v*, but one always sees *V* when writing in majuscules and *u* when writing in minuscules.

Now I do not say that this paleographic method of orthography which belongs to the golden age of Latin and which not a few among the learned have adopted is blameworthy or silly, but it does seem to me that the new forms (*J-j*, small *v* and capital *U*) that have not unreasonably come into use to make writing and reading easier and clearer are most useful, especially in the composition of a dictionary, and this I think no one can deny.

There are also people who, in the case of the genitive singular of those words that end in *-ium* or *-ius* (like *studium, beneficium, principium, Bonifatius, Ignatius*), do not double the *i* but end the noun in one *i* only (*studi, benefici, principi, Bonifati, Ignati*). In doing this they follow the practice that was in vigor, though not universally, during the time of the

---

7 *Id.*, I, 4, 10.
8 Cf. *Gramm.* I, 13; and I, 303.

Roman Republic, for it was only in the later time of the Roman Empire that an extra *i* was added for greater clarity.

Nor all this sort of thing is fine when one is quoting ancient codices and so must not change anything, but why should we use the same way of writing when we publish our books? Nor do I understand why a quicker and clearer way of writing, introduced profitably during the course of centuries, ought to be ignored and deprecated.

For orthography is a science that has progressed and continues to make progress in all languages that are written correctly,[9] and to reject this progress and revert to paleography is neither useful nor understandable nor right.

Why for example, do not a few reject the letter *j* but, on the other hand, use the letter *v*? If the former is rejected, then for the same reason so ought the latter, but if one of the two is accepted, it only makes sense that the other be as well.

I therefore follow many lexicographers[10] and not a few modern grammarians[11] when I use the small letters *j* and *v* when they stand for the consonantal use of *i* and *u*, and as for the genitive singular of those nouns ending in -*ium* and -*ius*, I have used the double *i*; all this I have done for one reason only, to adopt a clearer and more serviceable way of writing.

Finally, as everyone knows, the age of Cicero, in so far as Latin is concerned, was the Golden Age, but in the case of orthography—as Quintilian himself admits—its method was often uncertain and imperfect. One ought not, therefore, in a fit of pedantry, reject those developments that grammarians and scholars have, in the course of time, introduced.

---

[9] Suetonius writes the following about Caesar Augustus: "He has not so far adopted the orthography, that is, the way of writing, that the grammarians have recently adopted." (*Aug.*, 88)

[10] See, for example, Lewis and Short, *A Latin Dictionary*, and Eugène Benoist and Henry Goelzer, *Nouveau Dictionnaire Latin-Français*.

[11] See, for example, A. Gandiglio and G. B. Pighi, *Corso di Lingua Latina* (second edition), vol. I, pp. 4-10 and following.

IV. In the case of inscriptions, however, I have followed the best Latin writers not only of ancient but also of modern times and have used neither *U* nor *J*.

V. In the case of those words that are nowadays called *technical*, it usually happens that these are derived from a Greek source *parce detorta*[12] and that they plainly and clearly signify what is meant; nonetheless I almost always concocted a circumlocution—although not often sufficiently brief—to render those words somehow in Latin, supposing that to do so might at least prove to have some element of usefulness.

VI. Not a few of the best lovers of Latin—and these not only from Italy—especially Amleto Tondini, Karl Egger, Guglielmo Zannoni, and Pietro Bruno—have helped me correct the entries in this *Lexicon*. To all of them I publicly express my debt of gratitude.

After the publication in 1963 of the fourth edition of his dictionary, Bacci continued to coin new words and phrases for a future fifth edition, but *dira senectus* weighed heavily upon him, and his nephew and assistant Prof. Marsilio Bacci used to hear him say occasionally *Quod scripsi scripsi*, as if he was tempted to give up. Nevertheless by the time that his end was near, though no longer able to speak, he had produced twenty more pages of neologisms. These Marsilio Bacci published in *Latinitas* on the tenth anniversary of his uncle's death.[13]

Appearing in the same volume as the first edition of the Dictionary (1944) but subsequently, as I have noted, separated from it and published independently, was a volume of representative selections of Bacci's compositions entitled *Inscriptiones Orationes Epistulae*. Bacci, in his Introduction to the third edition of this work (1955), discussed the vexed question of what type of Latin should be used in the Catholic Church:

---

12   Horace, Ep. II, 3, 3.
13   Marsilio Bacci, *Vocabula nova ab Antonio Card. Bacci conscripta et nunc primum edita*, Latinitas, Rome, Typis Officinae "A Pace", March, 1981 (vol. I), 56–75.

Foreword

The third corrected and enlarged edition of this work is now being printed,[14] and I want to thank all to whom I owe thanks, who have privately in courteously written letters or publicly in reviews published in journals and newspapers praised the usefulness of these volumes more than they deserved. There were those who found something to censure, but they went about this gently and respectfully so that I had no reason—even in those cases involving suggestions that did not appear recommendable—to be angry with them or to be annoyed or displeased with their comments.

However, it is a good idea to mention here what does not seem to be sufficiently clear to everyone, namely, that there are distinct periods in the life of Latin: the earliest and best Latin commonly called *classical*, then Late Latin, next Latin in decline, and last of all Low Latin. All of these have their importance and their big and small uses. The Catholic Church employs all of these types of Latin on the appropriate occasions. Certainly she holds the best form of Latin in highest regard and commends it with all her authority, and she adorns her major documents with its harmony and elegance. When however it happens that matters must be dealt with more easily or more expeditiously, she does not refuse to use Late Latin so that everyone may understand her. She also borrows much from Christian writers that seems absolutely necessary in dealing with certain subjects.

In the Church's schools and universities instruction in sacred and profane subjects is generally delivered in that form of Latin derived from the authors of the Middle Ages which, although not an example of good Latin, has proven itself useful for the subjects with which it deals.

This I point out not in blame but in praise, for if the Church used only the ancient form of Latin that is called *classical* and should spurn all those words

---

14 In the third edition the work was divided into two volumes; the first of these contains the dictionary of modern words difficult to translate into Latin and the second the inscriptions, speeches, and letters.

that, though stigmatized as belonging to a later period, are necessary to describe new things,[15] then without doubt, with her as with other organizations, the Latin language would be held to be something dead, not something vital and useful. However it is precisely due to her willingness to make use of more than just classical language that it has turned out that Latin, after so many centuries and so many changes and vicissitudes, enjoys a certain permanence. And this happens not only in the groves of Academe, but in the very business of life, whenever the most ancient yet ever-living language of the city of Rome turns out to be the most noble instrument by which the Apostolic See can communicate its teachings, mandates, and admonitions to the universal church.[16]

This way of conducting business in Latin seems quite recommendable to those who respect that language not just as a venerable (though altogether extinguished) thing, but also as something yet living, strong, and most useful, for in our times when the diversity and confusion of so many languages divides our world and separates one nation from another, it alone can be, at least among educated men, an agreeable means of coming together and dealing with one another.

Nor should anyone say that this cannot happen because of most serious and absolutely insuperable difficulties, for what the Catholic Church is already doing must certainly not be thought impossible. Furthermore, no one really qualifies as a cultured man or as someone well educated, even in our times, who is altogether ignorant of Latin.

There is one other thing that seems worthwhile remarking which in my opinion not everyone understands clearly and perspicuously. There are certainly not lacking those who in their compositions so

---

15 See however what we have written in *Letter I* beginning on page 319 and in *Letter XIV* beginning on page 347.

16 Cf. Msgr. Antonio Bacci, *Il latino lingua viva nella Chiesa Cattolica*, extract from *Per lo studio e l'uso del latino*, Bollettino internazionale di studi-ricerche-informazioni, year II, n. 1; *Il Latino universale*, in *Ecclesia*, Rivista mensile, year V, n. 7, page 316 and following.

Foreword

intermingle and confuse the Latin of different periods — classical, late, declining, and low — that what flows from their pen is not something dignified or harmonious but rather something that is so distracting and irregular that it offends pious eyes and ears. Their method of composition reminds one somehow of the cloak of changing colors of the Venetian play and even brings to mind what Horace once said:

> *Humano capiti cervicem Pictor equinam*
> *jungere si velit et varias inducere plumas*
> *undique collatis membris, ut turpiter atrum*
> *desinat in piscem mulier formosa superne;*
> *spectatum admissi risum teneatis amici?*[17]

So, for example, they write *dependentiam, independentiam, competentiam, incompetentiam, plenarium, filialem, secretarium, respectivum, praecedentiam, Gubernium, visibilem, invisibilem,* etc., and together with these words from the late, declining, low, and barbarous periods, they mix in words and expressions from the most venerable age of the Latin language as if, by such ridiculous behavior, to endow their writings with some element of nobility. But these same people do not realize that they are sewing silk patches on rags! They would do much better if they held to the style of one and only one period throughout their composition, Late Latin or Low Latin. For how would people judge him who, when speaking and writing modern Italian, should mix up something from thirteenth century authors with something else from twentieth century authors? Certainly we ought to say and judge the same in the case of Latin.

I have tried to use the best Latin in this *Lexicon*, so far as my abilities permit, and since I certainly know that a goal of this sort cannot easily be reached, I ask your pardon, kind reader, and once again I beg of you

---

17 *Epist.*, II, 3. [If a painter chose to join a human head to the neck of a horse, and to spread feathers of many a hue over limbs picked up now here now there, so that what at the top is a lovely woman ends below in a black and ugly fish, could you, my friends, if favoured with a private view, refrain from laughing? (translated by H. R. Fairclough for the Loeb Classical Library)]

that if you find any mistake or inaccuracy, especially in the *Lexicon*, kindly share your opinion with me. Once again, farewell.[18]

Monsignor Bacci founded the journal *Latinitas* in 1953. One of the rules was that all articles had to be written in Latin: *Omnis tractatus sit latine scriptus.*[19] If a speech in Italian or French or any other modern language, even if by the Pope or another chief of state, was thought of such importance as to require publication in the journal, it was first translated into Latin for that purpose. In the same year Bacci started an annual prize contest, the *Certamen Vaticanum*, in which contestants submitted their compositions on prescribed topics. Advanced contestants competed for four prizes, two for prose and two for poetry. Younger contestants competed for two prizes, one for prose and one for poetry. The winners were celebrated at an annual ceremony in the Palazzo della Cancelleria. A small handful of cardinals particularly interested in Latin were always in attendance at this event; of these the most faithful were Giuseppe Pizzardo (1877-1970), Benedetto Aloisi Masella (1879-1970), and Fernando Cento 1883-1973). Bacci believed that Latin, not English, and in the case of the Roman Catholic Church certainly not Italian, was the wisest choice for the *lingua franca* of educated people from wheresoever in the world they might be. The reason for this is clear. For more than two millennia the civilized world was coextensive with the territory of the Roman Empire, in which the language of government was Latin. The Roman Catholic Church is in a real sense the successor of the Roman Empire. Without Latin one can understand nothing either of the Empire or of the Church; one is a man who does not

---

18 I have added not a few names of nations, regions, islands, and cities which, even though they were not used by the best Latin authors in ancient times or even known to them, are either not to be found in the common lexicons or are, if I am not mistaken, incorrectly given there.

19 *De Peculiaribus Horum Commentariorum rationibus et normis*, in *Latinitas*, vol. I, no. 1, page 9.

know his parents. This acceptance of Latin as the common language of all men was traditional until modern times, so the foundation is there. There is no such foundation for English, which until quite recently was a language of no importance for mankind as a whole. The renowned Latin experts Geneviève and Antonino Immè once wrote to me, *Nos vero Britannicam linguam omnino ignoramus.* — "We don't know any English at all." It is also not clear why the language of the English should be used, for example, by the French when they communicate with other peoples, and the French government has in the past resisted such an admission of subordination. Bacci discussed the goal and purpose of the journal *Latinitas* at the beginning of the first issue:

> To found a Latin journal, all of whose articles are to be written in Latin and which is to appear at stated times during the year is evidently not only a difficult undertaking but also somewhat precarious in our age, for there are few men today, even among the learned, who are sufficiently competent to write Latin compositions, nor, indeed, are there many who have the desire and determination to read them.
>
> There are certainly not lacking, either in Italy or in the other civilized countries, journals and periodicals, published at stated intervals, that knowledgeably, simply, and carefully deal with this subject, but most of these periodicals are only partly written in Latin, or even altogether composed in the languages of the countries where they are published.
>
> Our intention is to bring together all the best lovers of Latin, wherever in the world they may be, to join us, each according to his gifts, not only in interpreting and explaining, but also in restoring and renewing the Latin enterprise. For such a reason we determined to publish a journal in which the articles will obey the rule that whether written in prose or in poetry they have the authentic flavor of Latin and at the same time display its unique character and exalted dignity.

We are enthusiastic in raising this new torch of Latinity, for we are convinced that this means of speaking and writing is concise and flexible, rich and musical, elegant and dignified, not something whose lifeblood has flowed out, not inert, not dead, but living, still capable of bringing together men who delight in the study of humane letters and also suitable of so expressing and announcing the thoughts of out times that they can be understood by all people who are not unlearned. For no one is really learned who can not understand Latin.

As regards the usefulness of this renewal of Latin, we reckon as useful not only the diligent and skillful scrutiny of the writings of ancient authors, zeal for whose works flourished again after the middle period of the Roman language, but also those monuments of literature that the Catholic Church has raised down through the centuries, for apart from the fact that these works present teaching vastly surpassing that of the nations, they also convey their information in words that fit in neatly with divinely revealed truths and new productions of the human mind.

Some repeat again and again and rashly chatter—as was already babbled in past centuries—that the Latin language, just like an old hag, ugly, wrinked, toothless, and good for nothing, must be thrown out with disgust, since new languages, from whatsoever nations they have arisen, insofar as they have been accommodated to the use and knowledge of all, are already taking the place of Latin in common use.[20] There is no one who would deny the last part of the observation, nor do we disapprove of it, but the Roman language has something that the others lack, namely, that it is understood by the educated people of all nations, which certainly is not the case with the other various national languages, and for this reason it can serve as a bond of unity among the learned of all countries. Furthermore, it excels in such harmony of style and most lucid elegance, in such weaving

---

20 I. A. Aldini, *De vera latinae linguae fortuna*, Cesena, 1775.

Foreword

together of words and combining of sentences, as none of the modern languages possesses, so that the minds of them that study it are necessarily exercised and sharpened in the ability to judge and to reason.

Less far from the truth do they wander who claim — and these are today not few in number nor without the highest standing and influence — that they need only that amount of Latin required to read the authors of the classical and late periods and to explain them correctly, learnedly, and intelligently, but to study how to speak in the language of these same authors or to write it, a language not used or understood by all, is a vain and foolish thing, and those who do such a thing waste time and effort; wherefore just as the monuments of the fine arts should be most diligently preserved in museums and picture galleries for the admiration of tourists, so let the writings of ancient men be carefully catalogued and deposited in libraries and let them be accurately explained to students in the schools. Nothing further than this need be done in our age, in which men look for useful, convenient, and fruitful things rather than what is boring, though beautiful.

Now such observations as these are not without any shred of truth, but if we carefully examine them, they turn out to be not probable, not correct, but altogether false. For whoever should sedulously study enough of the Latin language as is required for him to understand Latin authors thoroughly and skilfully and thus enjoyably digests their style, their musicality, and the charms and pleasures they have to offer, will certainly not find it difficult to write in that same language nor unpleasing to read through the poems of some and the prose of others. This actually happened in that time when men of quality, who have since been called *humanists*, formed a sort of literary republic and happily brought it about that the study of the monuments of ancient literature should once again flourish even as they themselves produced new masterpieces worthy of comparison with the old. But if, as people keep on repeating, our times look for useful rather than beautiful things, then we must resist! The mind of man should not be content only with those things that are grasped by the senses as good but must fight for those delights of the spirit which proceed from the best literature and art.

We have therefore set out on this path of summoning all lovers of the Latin language, however many they may be, to join their energies and abilities with ours. We especially call out to men in sacred orders, for whom the study of the Latin language should be not only a duty[21] but also a glory.[22] Let them also remember that this musical language, even in our own age, has been declared by the Church to be its own, so much so that it can be called the Catholic language.[23] Let them also remember that it is a necessary bond whereby the different countries and their bishops are associated with the Roman Pontiff and by which the same Pontiff is connected with them. Thus, if this language is rejected or neglected, there is the danger "that the Christian religion, which ought to be one and simple, will become manifold and complicated, and be torn apart and divided into as many sects as there are languages.[24]

For this reason, the Supreme Pontiffs have more than once issued norms and admonitons that the "clergy, more than any others, be earnest in the study of Latin."[25]

There has never been a time when the Church has not promoted Latin studies. When the barbarian hordes, from here, from there, from many unknown places, rushed upon the Mother City, smashed the Roman Empire (which was already, as happens to all things human, drooping and then prostrate with age), and tried to reduce her to her old savagery, then the liberal arts and humane letters, like birds frightened

---

21 See the *Code of Canon Law*, 1364.2.
22 See Pius XII, *Allocutio ad Carmelitas habita*, Acta Apostlicae Sedis 1951, 737.
23 See Pius XI, Apostolic Letter *Officiorum Omnium*, Acta Apostlicae Sedis, 1922, 453.
24 I. Petrucci, *Oratio de lingua Latina revocanda et promovenda*.
25 Pius XI, Apostolic Letter *Officiorum omnium*, Acta Apostlicae Sedis, 1922, 453.

Foreword

and scattered by a sudden storm, sought protection in the cells of monks and there alone found a safe refuge. Similarly, as everyone knows, if during the dark and confused course of the Middle Ages, the monuments of Roman and Christian humanity, like the debris of a shipwreck, were saved for us, this must be attributed mostly to the clergy, who almost alone in those gloomy times cultivated the Latin language and taught it to others.

Now that a new humane culture has begun to flourish, so that not a few most learned men, brilliant in their command of the Latin language, are publishing books worthy of an eminent age, this too has happened under the patronage of the Church, which has greatly inspired and advanced the study of the best literature, as she has in the case of the other noble arts as well.

Why then do we not today raise high the glorious standard of Latin, passed on to us by our ancestors through the ages, and marching forward in the heat and through the dust, summon to it the students and devotees of this old and venerable language, however many of them there may be?

If we do this by our combined efforts, it may be hoped not only that the glory of Roman and Christian humanity, renewed by Latin literature, may shine again, but also that those nations, disturbed today by such bitter disputes and such smoking embers of controversy, may possess to their benefit this bond of unity and common mental culture.

Such was the program of Antonio Bacci. One of Bacci's axioms, that no one is truly learned who is ignorant of Latin and thus the learned of all nations know Latin, would be difficult to sell today on American college campuses, for about 99% of the population in the groves of Academe would fall into the category of the unlearned if this assumption were retained. It will be obvious to anyone who peruses a copy of the old *Latinitas* that it was a Catholic journal, yet there are many surprises to show that it was intended to cover all aspects of life. For example, in the twentieth anniversary issue there is a thirty-two page article by Reginald Foster giving a blow-by-blow account of the Joe Frazer-Cassius Clay heavyweight championship fight of "eight days before the Ides of March," 1971.[26] *Latinitas* continued as a Latin language journal for sixty years under the editorship of Bacci's successor as *Secretary of Briefs to Princes* Amleto Tondini (1953-1969), the preeminent Italian classicist Ettore Paratore (1969-1976), Bacci's old colleague the lexicographer Abbot Karl Egger (1976-1997), and finally Msgr. Anacleto Pavanetto (1997-2012), who was one of the chief Latinists at the Holy See during the period 1970-2001. In 1976 Pope Paul VI, observing with astonishment the collapse of Latin in the Church as a result of the vernacularization of the liturgy, scrambled to do something to undo the damage and issued the chirograph *Romani sermonis* by which he created the Vatican's *Latinitas* Foundation, under whose aegis the journal was placed. Pope Benedict XVI suppressed the *Latinitas* Foundation by the motu proprio *Lingua Latina* of November 10, 2012, replacing it with the *Pontifical Academy for Latin*; the first head of the new academy, Professor Ivano Dionigi, then took over the publication of a "new series" of *Latinitas*. This New Series publishes mostly articles written in the various modern languages, certain proof, if indeed one were needed, of the decline of Latinity at the Holy See. In fact, most of its articles, including the inaugural article of the New Series by the editor, are written in Italian. Once published four times a year, *Latinitas* now appears semiannually. Thus we observe in our own times the utter collapse of Latin in the Church of Rome, a catastrophe admitted repeatedly by Reginald Foster, who may be seen saying so in any number of *YouTube* videos; Foster was a prominent member of the Latin Letters Office of the Holy See in the period 1970-2009. Thus, through no fault of Bacci, the situation with regard to Latin, which had already deteriorated during the last decade

---

26 *Latinitas*, volume 21, number 2, September 1973, *Pugilatus certamen*, 141-172.

Foreword

of his life, has become a free-fall to rock bottom. Both in the academy and in the Church, Latin is no more. It survives as a pearl appreciated by a few but ignored by the many. It has been replaced by English in the secular world, and by Italian at the Holy See. The preponderance of Italian articles in the new series of *Latinitas* is thus in accord with the Italianization of the public face of the Catholic Church. The only significant Latin language journal still being published, as far as I am aware, is *Vox Latina* out of Saarbrücken.

Bacci's *Lexicon* contained no proper names, a deficiency that was made good by his colleague Karl Egger (1914–2003), who published his wonderful *Lexicon Nominum Virorum et Mulierum* in 1957.[27] Egger was born in Silz in the Tyrol province of the Austro-Hungarian Empire. He grew up farther south in Sterzing in that part of the province that was transferred to Italy after the First World War; Sterzing then became Vipiteno. He joined the Canon Regulars of the Lateran, entering their monastery at Gubbio in 1933. He was ordained a priest in 1937. Showing great promise in Latin, he studied at the Angelicum and Sapienza in Rome and was called to the Latin office of the Secretariat of State of the Holy See in 1949, where he rose to become Bacci's assistant. After the publication of his *Lexicon*, Egger became a titular abbot. At the death of Bacci, he became the foremost Latin scholar in the world. Here follows Egger's introduction to the first edition of his dictionary, with the addition of the last paragraph added for the second edition of 1963.

> Someone once said that there are already too many Latin dictionaries, some of which, composed by men famous for their abundant learning, are too complicated for anyone to derive much benefit from them while others, admittedly of more humble intellectual content, are quickly condemned to be forgotten.

---

27 *Lexicon Nominum Virorum et Mulierum*, Societas Libraria "Studium", Rome 1963.

We must, however, keep in mind that the work involved in writing dictionaries can never come to a successful conclusion unless whoever embarks on this enterprise adopts a more subtle strategy. For there is no book, no weighty opus, in which all Latin words and anything else that is pertinent are contained, especially if one takes into consideration the evidence of the manuscripts. So just as in higher studies, which the human mind can in no wise grasp as a whole, one scholar studies one subject and another scholar another, each investigating one above all others, a plan from which many useful discoveries have been forthcoming, so this specialization has proven productive even in writing dictionaries.

He therefore who wants to penetrate into the innermost sanctuary of Latinity must have available to himself specialized dictionaries like those restricted to the works of Cicero, to the Christian authors, to history, to archaeology, to mythology, and to the other branches of the study of antiquity, nor does he lack lexicons that treat of the use and choice of words in Latin composition such as the *Antibarbarus of* Johann Philipp Krebs (1771–1850) and, as regards the coining of new words, A. Bacci's *Lexicon eorum vocabulorum quae difficilius Latine redduntur.*

Since therefore such works are available, it seems desirable also to have a manual in which all the commonly received proper names of men and women are discussed in alphabetical order.

Of these not a few were employed by the ancient Greeks and Romans. Many more composed in the so-called Middle Ages were derived from a German source, or from some other, and others have appeared in a more recent age, often unscientific and yet accepted by both poets and novelists alike. The first sort have appeared in hefty editions crammed with specialized teaching that deal also with words from the field of geography. The others are usually found in titles written in the vernacular languages which, if they are translated into Latin, are discovered to have been done so quite idiosyncratically. For this

Foreword

reason, I have often dealt with the correct translation of certain names in the journal called *Latinitas*, and that not without the approval of the readers.[28]

Thus, having already, in a sense, begun this undertaking, I decided to write a dictionary of proper names, trusting that it would prove neither unpleasant nor useless to writers, speakers, and students of the Latin language and literature.

Here is the plan that I adopted in going about this enterprise: I collected only those names of men and women that are in use in our times, and it was no small concern of mine to determine the right way of writing up the entries so that they were founded on the best critical principles.

Since I was certain that it would be of no small help to readers, I have not neglected to show how to decline those names that come from Greek words.

I have furthermore tried, insofar as it was possible, to explain the etymologies of all the names, always mentioning the Indo-European root if the names sprung thence. For this my book seems to deserve commendation, since Cicero asserts, scarcely in error, "It is praiseworthy to give an explanation of the names, that is, how they came about, a science that is called *etymology*." [29]

In order that Latin lovers from all nations can use this book, vernacular names that are rendered into Latin are given not in one language only, but in many, even as many as five, if usage so requires.

Most male and female names are not restricted to one country only. The reader must not rebuke me if he should find that some name, though given in some languages, has not been given in his own language. This is a problem easy to solve since in almost all such cases we are dealing with forms of names that have some relationship one to another, so much so that the similarity can be noticed in the change from one language to another.

---

28 I, 1953, 308-311; II, 1954, 76-78; III, 1955, 62-66; IV, 1956, 63-64.
29 Acad. IV, 8; Varr. L. L., VII, 109; Quint., I, 6; Gell., XIX, 15.

ANTONIO CARDINAL BACCI

This book differs from those thick learned lexicons of Greek and Roman names that one finds hidden in the stacks of libraries as well as from those humbler tomes written in the vernacular languages in which less care is devoted to philological learning than to giving explanations of things that the individual names call to mind. Here and there I have made use of these volumes as indicated below.

My intention was not therefore to compose a sort of register or "voting list" of names but rather to bring forth from the workshops of philologists a little book for the use of those who speak and write Latin. This I certainly do not present to the public overconfidently, for I am aware that the material is varied and is not of the sort that it can ever be treated once and for all. This difficulty has nevertheless not prevented me from writing this dictionary, for as Cicero says,[30] "To one who has done all to win the first prize, the second or third prize is not dishonorable." [31]

What is written above was published as the preface to the first edition of this book, which was found so acceptable by its readers that all copies were quickly sold. It is now given to the public after having been slightly revised and with the addition of many more names.

Bacci sent the following letter of endorsement to be included in the preliminary matter of Egger's *Lexicon*:

---

30 *Or.* 1: *Prima sequentem honestum est in secundis tertiisque consistere.*
31 Against the system that I have adopted in accommodating German names to Latin ears, a passage from Morcelli has been quoted: "Nor would I recommend to you the method of certain people who, in order to express the names in the purest Latin, not only modify and inflect the last syllable, but molest others as well, so that what was once *Ruggerius* suddenly becomes *Rogerius*, and what was once *Gulielmus*, with the addition of new letters, is metamorphosized into *Willelmus*." (*De Stilo inscriptionum Latinarum*, II, p. 3, c. 1, n. 2.) Now Morcelli was a polished and elegant writer of Latin, but not a philologist, as becomes most evident when one looks at the examples he gives of names translated from German into Italian.

Foreword

While I was in the process of composing my *Lexicon* of words that are difficult to translate into Latin,[32] it occurred to me more than once to include the proper names of men and women which, received into use during the Middle Ages or in our own times, were not only *cinctutis non exaudita Cethegis*[33] but unknown even to the best ancient Latin writers, and today too it remains a matter of dispute how to spell them. But I had neither the possibility nor the strength to do so, and for this reason I exceedingly rejoice to see that you, after the most diligent study, the most tenacious labor, and with no common learning, have completed the work that I had hoped to accomplish myself.

I congratulate you for composing a book that is not only most useful but in a certain respect new. As everyone knows, there are several most accurate dictionaries of the names of men, women, regions, cities, rivers, and mountains, among which the most eminent for their weighty importance and deep erudition are those entitled *Onomasticon* written by Vincenzo De Vit (1810–1892) and Giuseppe Perin (1845–1925). However, in addition to the fact that there are not many who can have these weighty volumes readily available at hand, there is nothing in them which pertains to the more recent names of men and women, and so even the most learned men are stuck when it is a matter of rendering those names in Latin.

There is this additional reason for praising your book: In composing this *Lexicon* you always have in mind and bring into play the fact that philological and critical studies have made great progress in modern times so that in no wise can the well-known proverb be applied to your work, which is quite often said of that of others, *ex libris libri fiunt*.

What is more, the entries for the names listed in alphabetical order are so arranged that you first give them in Italian, then French, then Spanish, then English, and finally German, so that your dictionary is

---

[32] A. Bacci, *Lexicon vocabulorum quae difficilius latine redduntur*, fourth edition, Rome, 1963.
[33] Horace, *Epist.* II, 3, 50: "unrecognizable to the girded Cethegi".

useful even to readers who know only one of those languages. And certainly no man can be considered educated today, no matter where in the world he lives, who is altogether ignorant of every one of those languages.

You have therefore advanced in no small manner that which is the goal and the purpose of our journal *Latinitas*, to do as much as we can so that the Roman language, which exceeds all other ancient languages in the number of its speakers, its power, and its majesty, may not only thrive and flourish, but may become the common bond of unity among the learned of all mankind in the same way that it so happily is in the Catholic Church.

Egger provided Pius XII with a copy of his book, and the latter instructed Angelo Dell'Acqua, Montini's successor as *Sostituto* at the Secretariat of State (for he had subsequently been named Archbishop of Milan), to acknowledge the gift.

The present of your *Lexicon Nominum Virorum et Mulierum* was received by the August Pontiff with manifest sentiments of satisfaction and pleasure.

I am pleased to serve as the interpreter to your most reverend Excellency of the lively gratitude of His Holiness for this precious gift and for the latest proof of your filial and courteous regard for Him.

The importance of your long and accurate work, of which the *Lexicon* is the mature fruit, has not escaped His Holiness. The accurate Latin spelling of so many names of people of different origins and the easy way the contents can be used will in no little way interest the lovers of Latin, especially liturgists and drafters of documents in the Roman Curia.

Therefore it is the object of His august prayers that the work resulting from the competence and diligence of Your Excellency may effectively contribute to remove all uncertainty from writing and pronouncing Latin names and that it obtain for you the acceptance and agreement that it ought.

Foreword

> With best wishes for a happy reception of this book, the Vicar of Christ imparts to you and to the field of your activity the comforting Apostolic Benediction that always stimulates those who receive it to even more zealous labors.
>
> Acknowledging the copy so courteously presented to me, I take this opportunity to declare myself with special respect,
>
> Angelo Dell'Acqua
Sostituto

We now review briefly the history of Latin studies at the Holy See since the death of Cardinal Bacci in 1971.

Six years after Cardinal Bacci's death, Abbot Egger published his second great work, the *Lexicon Nominum Locorum* or *Dictionary of Place Names*.[34] A supplement containing an alphabetized list of all the Latin names of places treated in the *Lexicon* appeared in 1985. Egger's *Prooemium* is well worth study:

> Since I treated the subject of place names in the journal *Latinitas* quite often and not without the approval of the readers, it seems best to publish not only those explanations that have already appeared in print but also many others, all in alphabetical order in one book.
>
> The times in which we live do not favor an enterprise of this sort, but nevertheless enthusiastic students of Latin studies are not lacking, nor can we permit the light of these studies to be extinguished. There is the additional motive provided by the foundation *Latinitas*, recently established by Pope Paul VI to safeguard and increase the Latin language by appropriate neologisms.
>
> In composing this book, I have adopted the following rules:

---

34 *Lexicon Nominum Locorum*, Officina Libraria Vaticana, Libreria Editrice Vaticana (no date) with a supplement *Lexicon Nominum Locorum Supplementum Referens Nomina Latina Vulgaria*, Officina Libraria Vaticana, Libreria Editrice Vaticana 1985.

I. Only current geographic names are included in this lexicon, not ancient ones unconnected with modern life. Such ancient names can easily be found in other dictionaries. On the other hand, old names, even of the period of the decline of the Roman Empire, so long as, of course, they clearly and definitely apply to modern places, are retained. If there are no such ancient names, names from Mediaeval Latin or Low Latin (as it is called) are often sought.

II. Geographic names in modern languages, if not yet rendered into Latin, or poorly so, are prudently translated.

a) A current place-name that has a definite meaning is on occasion correctly changed into Latin or even into Greek if that is necessary. For example, Tel Aviv (= *collis vernus*) — *Vernicollis*; Addis Ababa (= *novus flos*) — *Neanthopolis*.

b) If this is impossible, the current name is accommodated to Latin ears — a thing the old Romans often did themselves — provided that good judgment is used and the character and dignity of the Latin language are kept in mind.

c) A current geographic name, if in no wise or scarcely capable of being given a Latin name, — again according to the example of the ancient Romans — is literally taken over as an indeclinable noun, for example, *Tingi* (= Tangier), Hebron, Bethlehem.

d) Once in a while a fitting composition is made by which two or three words coalesce into one. This often happens when the Greek word *polis* is added when places are named after a saint or a famous man, for example, *Francopolis* (= San Francisco) or, in ancient times, *Claudiopolis* and *Philippopolis*. It is known that the Romans, when combining words, usually joined together at most two of them but in the case of geographic names they sometimes combined three, for example, *Neoclaudiopolis*.

III. In accommodating foreign names to Latin ears I have not acted highhandedly but rather followed certain rules which had already come into force,

Foreword

especially those that are explained in Kraft's lexicon *Deutsch-lateinisches Wörterbuch, Geographischer Anhang*. Here follows a summary of these norms: The diphthongs *ei, ö, ü* of German names customarily become *i, o (oe), u* respectively. The French diphthongs *ai, ei, oi, oui* most often become *a, e, o, ue* respectively.

The final syllables of vernacular names are changed into Latin as follows:

ach, ack = *acum* or *achium*	*ey* = *ia* or *eia*
ad = *adum*	*feld* = *feldia*
agne = *ania*	*fels* = *felsa,*
ailles = *alia*	or it is translated
ain, eine = *ania, anium*	*ford* = *fordia*
al = *alium*	*furt* = *furtum*
au = *avia*	(rarely *fordia*)
aux = *atium*	*gart, garte,* = *gardia*
am = *amum*	*gorod, grod*
an = *ania* or *anum*	*gen* = *gia*
anz = *antia* or *antium*	*hausen,* = *husa* or *husium*
ar = *aria*	*husen, hus*
atz = *atium*	*haven* = *havia,* or it is
at = *atum*	translated
ig, ick, ich = *icus* or *icum*	*heim* = *hemum* or
ie = *ia*	*hemium*
ay = *aia* or *aria*	*hofen* = *hovia, hovium,*
berg = *berga*	or it is translated
born = *borna*	*holm* = *holmia*
burg = *burgum*	*holz* = *holtia* or *holtum*
cester = *cestria*	*horst* = *horstium*
dorf = *dorfium* or *dorpium*	*hum* = *humum*
e = *a*	*hut* = *hutum* or *huta*
eck = *ecca (eca)* or *eccum*	*igno* = *inium*
eglia = *elia*	*im* = *imum*
ein = *inum*	*in* = *inum*
em = *emum*	*inge, ingen* = *inga*
ence, en, enz = *entia*	*itz, itsch* = *itium*
er = *era*	*kirchen* = *kirka,*
euil = *olium*	or it is translated

land = *landia*	*pel, poli* = *polis*
leben = *leba*	sand = *sanda*
mold = *moldia*	stadt, städt, = *stadium*
mond, mont, = *montium*	statt
monte	stein = *stenum*
o (Italian, = *um*	tal, thal = *dalia* or *talia*,
Spanish,	or it is translated
Portuguese)	ton = *tonia*, rarely
oglio = *olium*	*tonium*
ogne = *onium* or *onia*	wegen = *vegia*
oping = *opia*	y = *ium*
oux = *usum*	zell = *cella*
ow = *ovia*	zza = *ssa*

IV. The names for the inhabitants of a place and the adjectives pertaining to foreign geographic names usually end in -*enses*, -*ensium*, and -*ensis*, -*ense* respectively. (In this lexicon the names of the inhabitants are given first, and then the adjectives.) I arrived at these endings by a study of 190 adjectives for old African place names. Of these, 134 ended in -*ensis*, 53 in -*itanus*, and three others with some different termination. But this is not an absolute rule since the ending -*anus*, -*a*, -*um* (and -*itanus*, -*a*, -*um*) is sometimes appropriately employed.

In the case of geographic names of two or more words (for example, *Portus Gratiae*, *Promunturium Viride*, *Urbs Lacus Salsi*), a short name for the inhabitants and a short adjectival form are not ready at hand. In these cases it is necessary either to use the genitive case or the ablative case after *de* or *ex* (for example, *civis Portūs Gratiae* or *templum Portūs Gratiae*).

V. A special difficulty arises when one must render foreign sounds that do not exist in Latin. The English combination of letters *sh* involving a sibilant (*sci*, *sce* in Italian, *ch* in French, *ch* in Spanish, *sch* in German), following the custom of the ancient Romans and Greeks, is usually rendered by *s* alone: Yerushalaim — Ierusalem, Yehoshuah — Iosue, Shêmuel — Samuel).

Foreword

The Italian sound *ci, ce* (*tch* in French, *ch* in Spanish, *ch* or *tch* in English, *tsch* in German) I have rendered into Latin somewhat boldly by *tz*. This combination *tz* is found in the Latin language, though not in the best Latin. Consider, for example, *Titzis*, the name of an Egyptian city in the *Antonine Itinerary*; *Tzoides*, a city in Thrace;[35] *Tzurulum*, mentioned by Procopius;[36] *Cutzara*, a woman's name;[37] *Cutzupitae* or *Cutzupitani*, found in Augustine[38] as a ridiculous name for the Donatists of Rome. For this reason I write Tzechoslovakia, following the modern Greeks, who write Τσεχοσλοβακία. In this regard, one must consider that the letter *z*, which came into the Latin language in the first century BC, was pronounced very sonorously as they now say, that is, quite sweetly. Evidence of this are the spellings *zmaragdus* (smaragdus) and *Zmyrna* (Smyrna) which are found in ancient literature. Those Germans and others err who pronounce this letter *z* in Latin just as they do in their own language, as an aspirate like *ts*. Thus, *tz* does seem to approach closely to that foreign sound that was described above.

That softer sound which also is made with hissing, that is, *ge, gi* in Italian, *dj* in French, *j* in English, *dsch* in German, is rendered by the combination *dz*. This combination, though rare, does indeed occur in Latin. Consider, for example, *Dzidzia*, a lady's name,[39] and *Dzoni*, a man's name (for *Dioni*).[40]

Obviously combinations of letters of this kind are used for foreign place names only, not for those that are derived from their ancient Latin appellations; compare, for example, *Nursia* (Italian Norcia) and *Perusia* (Italian Perugia).

---

35 A. H. M. Jones, *The Cities of the Eastern Roman Provinces*, Oxford, 1937, 25–26.
36 *Bell. Goth.*, III, 38.
37 *Corpus Inscriptionum Latinarum*, Berlin, VIII, 16039.
38 *Ep.* 53, 2
39 *Corpus Inscriptionum Latinarum*, Berlin, V, 7409.
40 *Corpus Inscriptionum Latinarum*, Berlin, V, 6215.

VI. The letter *w*, which is found frequently in the modern vernacular languages and even in Latin writings of the Middle Ages, is always rendered by the Latin letter *v*, which was the semi-consonant *u* (*uox*).

As for the letter *k*, it is customarily rendered *c* in Latin, but I have kept the *k* before the vowels *e* and *i* even in names that have been conformed to the Latin language, because of the variety of ways of pronouncing the combination *ce* and *ci* found among modern peoples.

As for the rest, the etymologies of place names have been provided whenever it could conveniently be done. However, all realize that this is an exceedingly complicated matter.

I send this work out confidently, trusting that it will prove of some utility to the lovers of Latin.

In 1992, under Egger's presidency, the Latinitas Foundation published the first volume (A–L) of the *Lexicon Recentis Latinitatis* or *Lexicon of New Latin Words*; the second volume (M–Z) appeared in 1997. A one volume edition appeared in 2003. The *Lexicon* was the work of sixteen people, of whom Egger was the *Moderator*. The fact that it was the work of a committee meant that it is not a discursive work as was the dictionary of Bacci; the entries in the *Lexicon Recentis Latinitatis* are generally much shorter than those of Bacci, who, like Dr. Johnson a sole author, could say what he wanted and was answerable to no one. Some discussion is allowed in the *Lexicon Recentis Latinitatis* when absolutely necessary; for example, in the entry *linciaggio* (lynching), after the definition *interfectio Lynchiana*, it is explained that the word is derived from the maladministration of justice by the American milita colonel Charles Lynch (1736–1786). Egger explained the reason for the composition of the *Lexicon Recentis Latinitatis* in his *Prooemium*:

> This *Lexicon* was originally begun because all copies of the dictionary of Antonio Bacci, *Lexicon vocabulorum quae difficilius Latine redduntur*, had been sold and that work was no longer in print. Furthermore, many

Foreword

new words introduced during the last three decades are not found in Bacci's book.

We have therefore determined to bring together many new words in two volumes and at the same time to include for the reader's benefit new entries that certainly belong in a Latin thesaurus but are not easy to find in the currently available dictionaries.

In coining new words we were careful to examine thoroughly the whole of Latin literature from the year 600 AD on. It must be observed that there are many more words in Late Latin than in the classical Latin of the Golden Age.

Whenever these sources were not available to us, we sought for words in the Latin of the Middle Ages, from Ecclesiastical Latin (which differs from the Latin of the Fathers of the Church), and from Greek, especially that currently in use. In cases when all these aids were lacking, then words truly new were coined, all the while keeping in mind the laws of philology and the character of the Latin language.

The preeminent source from which we drew the most was the *Thesaurus Linguae Latinae*, a truly outstanding work but still, alas, unfinished.

The words listed to be translated into Latin are Italian, but the text itself and all explanations inserted here and there are given in Latin.

As regards accents, short syllables are indicated only when they occur on the penultimate syllable in Latin words of three or more syllables; otherwise the accent in such words may be assumed to fall on the penult.

Etymologies are regularly given for all new words, especially those derived from Greek.

As much as possible we tried to translate Italian words into as few as possible Latin ones, preferably one. We had to keep in mind, however, that the Latin language is less able to combine several words into one than is the Greek.

As regards our method of citing the names of authors and their books of the period before the year 600 AD we have followed the method adopted by the *Thesaurus Linguae Latinae*. We have on purpose omitted the proper names of men and women as well as places names, and we refer the reader to the specialized dictionaries that treat of those topics.

Certainly some of Bacci's definitions needed to be adjusted to current circumstances. For example, he had followed Pope Leo XIII in defining *protestants* by *novatores* and had added the option *haeretici novatores*. Although the *Lexicon Recentis Latinitatis* has the full complement of entries necessary to make it serviceable to the functionaries of the Roman Curia, it is intended to be of use in all aspects of modern life; so, for example, the lover of coffee will find here all the technical vocabulary necessary to place an order (even for the most specialized potion) at *Starbucks*. Unfortunately, the years following the publication of the *Lexicon Recentis Latinitatis* were years of further decline of Latin at the Holy See. By the time at the end if the twentieth century when Anacleto Pavanetto (1931–2021) was in charge of the Latin Office of the Secretariate of State, documents to be translated into Latin would be divided up among several translators, one section to each, so that the result was clearly not the work of one man. For this and other reasons, Reginald Foster remarked that among the German scholars, the reputation of the Vatican Latinists was low.

In the year 2021 we observed the fiftieth anniversary of the death of Antonio Cardinal Bacci (January 20). The learned world will long admire the excellence of his linguistic achievements. We conclude by examining the lasting influence that his work has had on the life of the mind. If we look at the current situation with regard to the two main elements of his program, we might at first despair. Those two doctrines were, first, that the Latin language should be the medium of communication among the learned of all nations, and second, that the Latin language should be the Catholic language, the official language of the Church for the transaction of business and for the celebration of its liturgy. In the eyes of the world, the cause of Cardinal Bacci went down to defeat. What is the most that can be hoped for in the present circumstances, the best that can be done?

That the Latin language is unknown to the overwhelming majority of the people who number themselves among the learned is obvious; today, if an author wants his composition to be read, he will write it in English. The cause of Latin as the universal common language of the educated is lost; that role is now assumed by English. The consequences are tremendous and were predicted by Schopenhauer (1788-1860):

> The abolition of Latin as the universal language of learned men, together with the rise of that provincialism which attaches to national literatures, has been a real misfortune for the cause of knowledge in Europe. For it was chiefly through the medium of the Latin language that a learned public existed in Europe at all—a public to which every book as it came out directly appealed. The number of minds in the whole of Europe that are capable of thinking and judging is small, as it is; but when the audience is broken up and severed by differences of language, the good these minds can do is very much weakened. This is a great disadvantage; but a second and worse one will follow, namely, that the ancient languages will cease to be taught at all. The neglect of them is rapidly gaining ground in France and Germany.
>
> If it should really come to this, then farewell, humanity! Farewell, noble taste and high thinking! The age of barbarism will return, in spite of railways, telegraphs and balloons....
>
> To be entirely ignorant of the Latin language is like being in a fine country on a misty day. The horizon is extremely limited. Nothing can be seen clearly except that which is quite close; a few steps beyond, everything is buried in obscurity. But the Latinist has a wide view, embracing modern times, the Middle Age and Antiquity; and his mental horizon is still further enlarged if he studies Greek or even Sanscrit.

> If a man knows no Latin, he belongs to the vulgar, even though he be a great virtuoso on the electrical machine and have the base of hydrofluoric acid in his crucible.
>
> There is no better recreation for the mind than the study of the ancient classics. Take any one of them into your hand, be it only for half an hour, and you will feel yourself refreshed, relieved, purified, ennobled, strengthened; just as if you had quenched your thirst at some pure spring. Is this the effect of the old language and its perfect expression, or is it the greatness of the minds whose works remain unharmed and unweakened by the lapse of a thousand years? Perhaps both together. But this I know. If the threatened calamity should ever come, and the ancient languages cease to be taught, a new literature shall arise, of such barbarous, shallow and worthless stuff as never was seen before.[41]

The reintroduction of Latin into the curriculum of the college courses of the commonality of high schools can only be accomplished if demanded by the parents and students; the initiative will not come from the current class of teachers, administrators, and school boards. In the secular realm, the loss of Latin is correlated with the collapse of grammatical knowledge. Like the Emperor Sigismund, the people of today hold that they are above grammar; there is no respect for it.[42] As a result modern books are generally insufferable to read. The failure to recognize the primary meaning of words like *man* and *he*, the use of *they* as a singular pronoun, and the loading of children for life with bizarrely spelled names are signs of a time most unwelcoming to the Latin mentality. An infallible sign of this educational disease is the fact that the children and grandchildren of many of you reading this page are not being taught in the public schools how to

---

[41] *On the Study of Latin*, in: *The Art of Literature* by Arthur Schopenhauer, translated by Thomas Bailey Saunders, https://en.wikisource.org/wiki/The_Art_of_Literature/On_the_Study_of_Latin.

[42] "Ego sum Rex Romanorum et super grammaticam."

Foreword

sign their names legibly or how to read cursive handwriting, knowledge that was formally imparted in the first grade. There is furthermore unfortunately prevalent the idea that education in the humanities need not be founded upon the masterpieces of literature. If people are not educated on the basis of Shakespeare and Milton, why should they care about Cicero or Vergil? Thus, the study of the humanities as taught in modern high schools, colleges, and universities is pointless and even counterproductive. What can be done? In my own town people of culture under the leadership of a local physician demanded that their children be taught Latin in the public high school. *Mirabile dictu,* they succeeded. When the doctor died, Latin was once again removed from the curriculum. From this episode I conclude that there is some hope of success in cases where the people take a firm stand. There is the additional problem that teaching in our times is not a profession held in esteem or remunerated at a sufficient level to attract the best people. One becomes a teacher when one fails at everything else or loses an election. This situation may never be remedied until things deteriorate to the point that it is realized that the very survival of the country is at stake and that the United States has been left in the dust. Those fortunate and intelligent enough to have learned Latin will keep the language alive among themselves and promote it in the general population so that we are ready for the day when its value becomes more widely appreciated. In this they will be inspired and assisted by the example and work of Cardinal Bacci.

Within the *una sancta catholica et apostolica ecclesia*, the effects of the situation in society at large and of the liturgical changes of the 1960's has resulted in a similar collapse. The abolition of Latin has resulted in the removal of the *mysterium tremendum et fascinans* from the Catholic religion. One must search diligently to find a church where the Mass is celebrated in Latin, even in Rome; Latin has simply disappeared, an event human all too human, but officially brought about (some say) by the direct inspiration of the Holy Ghost. Pope Francis avoids Latin and gives the impression that he considers it a nuisance or an evidence of obscurantism. The reemergence of Latin in the Roman Church would require a recognition, not felt today but on the contrary rejected at the highest levels, that the Latin language is essential for the identity of a Catholic, that without the Latin language, the Catholic Church is something different from what it used it be, that with the collapse of Latin something necessary for the survival of the religion, not something secondary, has been lost. The foolish suppose that the Latin language has nothing to do with the essence of the Catholic religion, but this is an error. The close correlation between the authority of the Roman See and the use of the Latin language was maintained by Dr. Döllinger (1799-1890), who said:

> The time is coming when Latin will cease to be the language of Catholicism, and with the cessation of Latin much of the power of Rome will go.[43]

To become a priest in the Catholic Church today, it is no longer necessary to have the slightest knowledge of the Latin language. As a result, the clergy insensibly acquire the idea that the Catholic religion is a modern phenomenon that can be adjusted to the assumptions of the times. Since Latin is difficult to learn, the standard of education of the clergy is significantly lowered by removing the requirement of competence in that language. The result is a clergy consisting in general of humbly educated people. These eventually become bishops, cardinals, and popes. Of course, Christ himself did not impart his teachings in Latin, nor must one understand Latin in order to ascribe to them, but the Latin language is an inconvenient obstacle to anyone who would modernize a verse or tamper with a doctrine.[44] With regard to the rites of the Church, the

---

43 Ignaz von Döllinger, in Alfred Plummer, *Conversations with Dr. Döllinger, 1870-1890*, edited with Introduction and Notes by Robrecht Boudens, Leuven University Press, page 15.
44 I am thinking here of the English translations "for all men" and then

collapse of Latin is the hydrogen bomb on the sacred liturgy. The quality of the public ceremonial of the Church has in a period of sixty years been reduced to zero. The cause of Latin as *the* Catholic language can be saved, but this depends on the survival of the Latin liturgy; otherwise, it too is lost. The promotion of the Latin liturgy is rendered more reasonable by the value of the Latin Church music, a gigantic marvel of civilization compared to which the English Church music is a dwarf. The Catholic Church is the last existing institution with an obvious and strong connection with Latin; the promotion of Latin within the Church is thereby undeniably Catholic. It is the modern tendency to dismiss and suppress Latin that is a noticeably foreign element in the Church. These advantages make the campaign for Latin a beautiful struggle with a great hope of success. Cardinal Bacci warned about all the inevitable consequences of the fall of Latin. He knew the meaning of his profession. Had he condescended to use Late Latin, he could have said *Dixi et salvavi animam meam*. He left behind a magnificent monument of Latin learning and an edifying example of loyalty to a noble cause.

Anthony Lo Bello
March 28, 2021

"for all", which were introduced into the Mass by people who did not dare to change *pro multis* to *pro omnibus*.

INTRODUCTION

For many years the *Banca del Mugello*, formed on December 31, 1972 by the merger of the rural banks of the towns of Piancaldoli, Coniale, and Luco di Mugello, has been giving special attention to sponsoring, whether in collaboration with others or by itself, publications devoted to the history, noted personalities, and local traditions of the places in which it operates.

I could not allow to pass, therefore, on this, the anniversary of the centenary of the founding on November 6, 1910 of the Rural Savings and Loan Association of Piancaldoli, the opportunity to provide the funds for the publication of a volume about Antonio Cardinal Bacci, born in 1885 in Giugnola, the founding partner who became famous throughout the world for his deep knowledge of Latin, which he learned first of all in the school of the archiepiscopal seminary of Firenzuola, where the Archbishops of Florence had invited experienced instructors to teach literary and scientific subjects.

Today, the general management, the board of directors, and the Firenzuola branch of the Banca di Mugello's cooperative credit offices have their seat in the communities reorganized as a result of the destruction of the whole area caused in the bombardment by the Allied air forces on September 1, 1944.

The name *Antonio Bacci* appears as a founding partner among the names of the "pioneers of cooperative credit" in the document establishing the Rural Savings and Loan Association of Piancaldoli.

His fame is due almost entirely, it is true, to his exceptional knowledge of Latin, the language in which he wrote the official documents of the Church for four Popes.

However, in a time of usury, of extremely high interest rates charged for loans to farmers by unscrupulous wealthy people of that money-making and money-amassing middle class, the sensibility of the local clergy and, therefore, of Don

Bacci favored the rise of the small local banking enterprise in the little outlying communities of Piancaldoli and Giugnola, located *in Etruriae Aemiliaeque finibus*, on the border of Tuscany and Emilia.

By its commitment, the clergy repeatedly demonstrated its innovative spirit, its attention to the needs of the people, its culture, and its reputation for fairness in which men and women placed their absolute trust, finding there complete moral and, in this case, financial support. In fact, the Rural Banks are the tangible expression of the Christian and social conscience of quite a large part of the clergy.

The pages of this book are meant to be an act of homage to the figure of the great Latinist Antonio Cardinal Bacci, but they also intend to represent that testament of thanks for his having made his own contribution, together with the Provost Don Francesco Pifferi and all the other members of the initial shareholder structure, so that one hundred years ago there could be born the little bank that is still active, along with its subsidiaries, in the communities of the Mugello, at Sesto Fiorentino and at Florence, as well as in the border towns of the Emilia Romagna and of the province of Prato.

Paolo Ruffini, Accountant
President of the Board of Directors
(*Banca del Mugello Credito Cooperativo*)

FROM THE EDITOR

ON JANUARY 25, 2010 I HAD THE OPPORTUnity to make the acquaintance of Monsignor Loris Capovilla, once secretary to Pope John XXIII, when I visited him in the company of editor Gabriele Angelini, who at the time was in deep mourning for the loss of his fourteen year old son Filippo; the purpose of our visit was to obtain from that prelate the preface for a volume with the title *Vergine bella che di sol vestita* consisting of collected praises and invocations to the Blessed Virgin Mary during the course of the history of Italian literature. It was an overwhelming visit to Sotto il Monte which I shall never forget, in rooms full or memories and documents, during which the "little bishop" (as he often liked to call himself) seemed to me to breathe in conversation the clean air rich with that simple, clear and friendly frankness, typical of men of faith, which brought me back in memory to the evangelical welcoming manner and convincing way of speaking of my pastor of many years past. In a second meeting, during which we presented him with the first proofs of the above-mentioned book, I mentioned to the Archbishop that we were then celebrating one hundred years since the founding of the Rural Bank of Piancaldoli, among whose founding partners had been Don Antonio Bacci, who became thereafter a personality famous for his elegant Latin and his service to four Popes (including John XXIII). Since, by decision of the *Banca del Mugello*, the direct descendant of the Rural Banks of the same area, funds were to be provided for a publication about that individual, I dared to ask him, who had certainly known Bacci well, to write some pages on the "Secretary of Briefs to Princes" who had been elevated to the purple by the good Pope, to be included in the book which was to be sent to the press before the end of the year. My request found favor with Loris Francesco Capovilla, who, with joy at being able to make himself useful, placed himself at my immediate disposal. I express to him my own feelings of profound gratitude as well as those of the whole family of the *Banca del Mugello*, for having enriched by his contribution the publication rendering homage to the figure of him who, *latinitatis cultor et amator*, gave luster in the whole world to the Church and to his region of origin.

Pier Carlo Tagliaferri

LETTER OF HIS EXCELLENCY
LORIS FRANCESCO CAPOVILLA

Sotto il Monte Giovanni XXIII
May 23, 2010
Feast of Pentecost, Alleluia

Pier Carlo Tagliaferri
Via San Pellegrino 375
50033 Firenzuola, Florence

Dear Pier Carlo,

1. Divine Providence has disposed that the death on November 17, 2008 of the radiant teenager Filippo Angelini from Sasso Morelli and our participation in the mourning of his parents Livia and Gabriele — a heartbreaking and edifying event to be recalled and retold with broken words and long pauses — caused us to meet one another and, in the warmth of sympathy and shared cultural interests, we encouraged one another in doing good in the service of humanity and we dreamt of that widening of human relationships that renders less difficult the slow road to the "new land in which justice has its fixed residence" (2 Peter 3, 13), a residence that incorporates truth, goodness, and beauty.

Thanks to you I renewed my memories of two fellow countrymen of yours, the layman Tito Casini and the priest Antonio Bacci, the former inscribed among the teachers of our maternal Italian language, the latter among those of the Latin of the Golden Age.

When I was fifteen years old, I came to know Casini through his enchanting books, and now, in the hour of vespers, just by listing some of them, my eyes swell up with tears: *La bella stagione, La vigilia dello sposo, I giorni del ciliegio, Il poema dei Patriarchi*, and *Il pane sotto la neve* (1929-1935). These pages strengthened my faith, introduced me into the sanctuary of the liturgy, and convinced me to familiarize myself with the Book *par excellence* and to mull over each of its words, so much so that since then I have always avoided drinking at the polluted fountains of false culture.

I knew the other, Antonio Bacci, since 1958, the first year of my apprenticeship in the Vatican. I realized at once that he was a priest, a priest of the Mass, of the Breviary, of those solid devotions enriched with teachings from the Gospels, a priest of unconditional service to the Holy See, a prelate known and prized by the Supreme Pontiff, by the Roman Curia, and by the Italian and foreign cultural organizations, a theologian and patristic scholar, a humanist and a philologist, a man of obvious intellectual depth, determined to walk in the path of the beatitudes, holy and strict, an amiable custodian, patient and at everyone's disposal, able to remain on the job throughout the night without exhaustion or worry. For forty-seven years his *Lexicon eorum vocabulorum quae difficilius latine redduntur* has been at my side, and I consider myself a student of this great teacher. As I meditate on his course of life and on his literary productivity, and as I think about how many writings of his must still lie unedited in the archives, I once again feel the vibrant and seductive affirmation of the apostle, "True faith is useful to everyone," (I Timothy 4, 8); it is the faith that emanates from *pietas*. On this charism that consecrates and inflames everything, Don Giuseppe De Luca, the priest who in the twentieth century honored the Church of Rome more than all others, flew high and placed in our hands the key that opens the door to the sublime, to the

Letter of His Excellency Loris Francesco Capovilla

inexpressible, to the eternal. There are sixty-six pages which I would consecrate to the cardinal Antonio Bacci and the author Tito Casini, men of God, "pilgrims of the Absolute" (Léon Bloy), "beggars of heaven" (Jacques Maritain). They are to be found just as I have described them in the detailed work of De Luca.[1]

2. There is attributed to John XXIII the evangelical aphorism, "I seem to be an empty sack that the Holy Ghost unexpectedly fills up with strength." It is likely that Casini and Bacci thought the same way, instructed by the Apostle Paul, "If one imagines to be something, when he is nothing, he fools himself (Galatians 6, 3)." People of that sort, learned and reserved, researchers and creators, are at the same time supreme artists and humble artisans.

Following the logical and historical thread that binds me to Pope John, I share without reservation the judgment concerning his *pietas* and culture that Cardinal Giacomo Lercaro made, and I feel compelled to place by the Pope's side the two figures of Bacci and Casini with whom I have become fascinated. What follows is a page that says it all and says it perfectly.

> One can make a distinction among the aforementioned men of culture. There are those that create culture, who disseminate it and are its mediators, and there are those who consume it to an eminent degree and in an eminent manner. The former can be very different from the latter, and it is possible (and it very often happens) that a creator of culture seems to be without culture himself to the mere consumers of culture. However, no one can be a creator of culture by inspiration of the Most High without having arrived, at least with some effort of his own, at a necessary and very deep assimilation of the vital elements of a great cultural tradition.
>
> This distinction does not necessarily hold always, but it is often coincident with another distinction that is particularly valid in the realm of Church culture.

---

[1] *Archivio italiano per la storia della pietà*, vol. I, Rome, 1951, *Edizioni di storia e Letteratura*, Introduction.

There are first of all the men of the Sources who educate themselves if not entirely at least mainly by a thorough and thoughtful familiarity with the great Sources of Christianity, the Scriptures, the Fathers, and the Saints who have characterized a Church or an epoch. Then there are the men whose education is based on textbooks who, in the best of cases, themselves arrive at the production of a quite successful textbook, and finally there are the men formed primarily on the basis of essays and monographs, who are too intelligent and discriminating to be content with a textbook but who are not sufficiently learned to be able to feed mainly upon the original sources. The first remain in many cases within normal confines and can then be quite worthy scholars or sincere and influential educators with a certain solidity, freshness and originality; in this case they attain a transcendent force and are thus the creators who, having gone back into the past so far as to reach the sources at their most mysterious and living origin, can, with a great jump, anticipate the future. They are the men, in conclusion, whose learning is timeless and if anything is the learning of the future. The second class of men, those of the textbook, even in the most extreme examples, are the men of the "present perfect" who have succeeded a little in comprehending the past and almost rendering it present, though not without losses (even serious ones), mutilations, and simplifications. The third class of men, finally, are the true men of the present, the immediate present, whose less profound foundation often leads to practical limitations. Sensitive to the influences of day-by-day modern life, they often embrace its forms and its terminology, but, not having sufficiently penetrated into the depth of the sanctuary in which Tradition hides its mysterious and most profound face, they cannot find conviction and strength to make the most difficult, the most liberating, and the most prophetic choices.

It is possible that the culture of the first type of men arrives at such a degree of essentiality that it only reveals itself to those who are in some way synchronized with them and capable of comprehending innately. Very often the man who arrives at this level makes himself a creator of culture without many of his contemporaries noticing it and even without he himself noticing it, because his culture is so limpid and pure a recovery of the creative tradition that it ignores itself and is incapable of any reflection on itself.[2]

3. John XXIII became a creator of culture in the highest and most obvious meaning of the word precisely because, from his teenage years and for decades afterwards, he let himself be instructed by *ratio et fides* and completely surrendered himself to the activity of the Spirit; he nourished himself not with unstable fantasies but with *obedience and peace*. We can imagine him, at twenty-three years of age, (at the beginning of his priesthood), entering the realm of that *peace and liberty* described in the golden little book *The Imitation of Christ*:

> My Son, now will I teach thee the way of peace and of true liberty. Do, O my Lord, as Thou sayest, for this is pleasing unto me to hear. Strive, My Son, to do another's will rather than thine own. Choose always to have less rather than more. Seek always after the lowest place, and to be subject to all. Wish always and pray that the will of God be fulfilled in thee. Behold, such a man as this entereth into the inheritance of peace and quietness. O my Lord, this Thy short discourse hath in itself much of perfectness. It is short in words but full of meaning, and abundant in fruit. For if it were possible that I should fully keep it, disturbance would not so easily arise within me. For as often as I feel myself disquieted and weighed down, I find myself to have gone back from this teaching. But Thou, Who art Almighty, and always lovest progress in the soul, vouchsafe more grace, that I may be enabled to fulfil Thy exhortation, and work out my salvation.[3]

---

2 Cardinal Giacomo Lercaro, *John XXIII — Linee per una ricerca storica*, Rome, 1965, Edizioni di Storia e Letterattura, 23-25.
3 Book III, chapter 23, §§ 1-4, translated by Rev. William Benham

Inclined as I am by nature and by education to connect together the adventures of the saints and the heroes, of the wise at heart and the sleepless seekers after truth, I have deliberatively come to the conclusion that only the man who has stripped himself of all, like the *Kenosis* of the Son of God, sings the victory paean.

Tito Casini and Antonio Bacci, my friends—so I feel them to be and call them—deserve to be placed in the Olympus of creators, so much the more because the amorous and nostalgic elegy of Giuseppe Parini to the village folk suits them:

> That is on earth true fame,
> If we can leave a name
> For all eternity,
> A lasting memory. (*La Vita Rustica*, 1790)

4. The *Banca di Credito Cooperativo di Mugello*, served so well and wisely directed by men who love our region, history, tradition, and archives, will know how to preserve the inheritance of its champions and how to increase its reputation by favoring the dissemination of its still hidden treasures. And it is natural that this praiseworthy attitude, fully acknowledged, shine once again and increase even more on this centenary of the *Istituto di Credito*.

To conclude, dear Tagliaferri and dear friends of Firenzuola, let me pick a flower from the garden of John XXIII and deposit it with you on the altar of the Blessed Pope and on the graves of the wonderful people being piously remembered in your book.

On the evening of May 31, 1959, Pope Roncalli wrote on a scrap of paper at hand the following diary-like note:

> This was a rather busy and, I hope, fruitful day. I celebrated Holy Mass, and there were edifying communicants. My closing words. Complete happiness. O Mary, Queen of Heaven, thank you. There followed two crowded audiences in the Hall of Benedictions. In the evening a walk in the gardens with Monsignor Bacci...[4]

---

[4] John XXIII, *Nostra pace è la voluntà di Dio*, Saint Paul editions, 2001.

Letter of His Excellency Loris Francesco Capovilla

Noteworthy among the meetings of the day was an audience for the new Confederation of Canons Regular of St. Augustine, where he gave an address that had been translated into elegant Latin by Monsignor Bacci, at that time still in the Secretariat for Briefs to Princes. Our Latinist came up with the suggestive title *Fausti eventus*, and he introduced into the text an appropriate passage from St. Augustine:

> Strive to cultivate with the utmost diligence and with reciprocal emulation that commandment that you have embraced. Love truth, maintain unity, foster charity, through which the other virtues flourish and with which nothing that belongs to the really good can be lacking. And in order that you may be able to attain the highest level of religious perfection, I exhort you with the words of St. Augustine himself: In the fervor of the Spirit set yourselves afire from the flame of charity, that it may make you fervent in the praises of God and in exemplary conduct of life. Is one warmer but the other not so much? Let him who is warm set the tepid one on fire. Let him who has less ardor crave an increase and pray to obtain fraternal assistance. (Sermon 5, Easter time, 3)

For my own part I add the wish that on those tiresome, unproductive, turbulent days, we lift up our eyes unto the hills, repudiate mediocrity, be cognizant of our baptismal promises, strive to "serve fatherland and humanity disinterestedly" (Dag Hammarskjöld), remain in certain expectation of the radiant morning star that is Jesus (Apocalypse 22, 16), and not give ourselves up to fear or pessimism.

> *Tantum aurora est.* We are at the beginning of that period of evangelization and civilization that takes its name and life blood from Christ (John XXIII, October 11, 1962, opening address to the Second Vatican Council).

And the Church to which we have the honor to belong? What about the Church? The Christian educated in the school of the Second Vatican Council does not fear and does not back off. The believer affirms with the Apostle Paul that the Church is *sine macula et sine ruga* (Ephesians 5, 27). Beautiful and young, humble and merciful.

> Men can certainly fail the Holy Ghost, but the Holy Ghost can never fail the Church. Our worst infidelities will never separate her from the love of God which is in Jesus Christ. With her testimony and with her inalienable powers, she will always be the sacrament of Jesus Christ. She will always make Him really present. By means of the best among her children, she will never cease to reflect His joy. When she seems to show signs of weakness, a secret germination prepares new spring times for her, and in spite of all the obstacles that we put up, saints will always continue to be born. [5]

Dixi humiliter et simpliciter. I have stammered on but with humility and conviction. Thank you for reading this. Thank you for once again exchanging expressions of respect, esteem, and affection, which I reciprocate to all of you. Let me speak like a Roman, with best wishes for good and happy days full of hard work and results: *Quod bonum, felix, faustum, fortunatumque sit.*

Loris Francesco Capovilla
Archbishop of Mesembria,
(the titular archdiocese of
Angelo Giuseppe Roncalli
in the period 1934-1953)

---

[5] Henri De Lubac, *Meditazioni sulla Chiesa, L'Osservatore Romano*, May 25, 1996.

I
Antonio Cardinal Bacci
BIOGRAPHICAL NOTES
by Nello Lascialfari

FROM FIRENZUOLA TO ROME

Antonio Bacci was born in Giugnola-Castel del Rio in the diocese of Florence on September 4, 1885. In 1909, after having completed his studies and earned his degree in theology at the seminary of Florence, he was ordained a priest.

The high level of preparation which he attained in his studies and especially his great love for Latin letters won widespread respect and acknowledgment. In fact, Alfonso Cardinal Mistrangelo, Archbishop of Florence, immediately appointed him to the faculty of the seminary at Firenzuola with the rank of professor, and he was subsequently promoted to be the seminary's director. In 1921 the Cardinal determined to send him to Rome to enter the service of the Secretariat of State, where he was appointed to the position of Latin *minutante*, an office which he fulfilled with great learning and dedication for over nine years.

In 1931, following the death of Cardinal Galli and of his successor Monsignor Sebastiani, the office of Secretary of Latin Briefs to Princes became vacant, and it was Antonio Bacci who was called to fill the position. His profound knowledge of the Latin language got him this just recognition which required him to compose the principal and most important documents during the pontificates of Pius XI, Pius XII, and John XXIII. In 1944 among his responsibilities was to give the funeral eulogy of the Secretary of State, Luigi Cardinal Maglione.

Upon the death of Pope Pius XI in 1939, the Sacred College entrusted him with the responsibility of writing and reciting the funeral oration and later the *oratio pro eligendo pontifice*, the oration before the election of the next Pope.

He similarly composed the funeral oration after the death of Pius XII, and one must particularly recall the *oratio pro eligendo pontifice* given at the Mass *de Spiritu Sancto* at the opening of the conclave of 1958, in which John XXIII was elected. In this speech, Bacci made an acute examination of the situation in the Church and in the world and he indicated with almost prophetic wisdom the virtues and the program which proved to be those of the future pontiff.

In the consistory of March 28, 1960, Pope John XXIII elevated him to the dignity of Cardinal Deacon with the title of Sant'Eugenio alle Belle Arti, a basilica erected with offerings from the whole world on the occasion of the episcopal jubilee of Pius XII. On April 19, 1962 he was consecrated bishop at the hands of Pope John himself as required by the new *moto proprio* according to which all the cardinals should be bishops.

Cardinal Bacci is above all known as a Latinist. For him Latin was not merely an object of study, learning, or academic exercise, but a second language, and he always considered it living, vital, and necessary for every cultured person. Latin as the official language of the Church was his language, and the Supreme Pontiff used it to communicate the teachings of the Church to the whole Catholic world, teachings that involve not only the ideas, problems, and things of the past but also of the age in which we live. For this reason, and especially on account of his official position, helped by the ease of expressing himself in Latin acquired in so many years of work and study, he forged new words and phrases as well as some expressions, particularly difficult to get right, that he introduced in the most important documents that dealt with such varied things as dowsing, the radio, television, cinema, and all the most recent scientific and technical inventions.

Making use of this long experience, Bacci edited and published many works in Latin. Among the most important is the *Vocabolario italiano-latino delle parole moderne* of over 700 pages, which went into many editions, as well as a volume of Latin compositions entitled *Varia latinitatis scripta*.[1]

He was a man of fervid piety and of exalted spirituality, and in this connection he published, especially for the young, a book of *Meditazioni per tutti i giorni dell'anno* as well as various works of asceticism and mysticism.

For twenty-seven years he also held the position of datary of the Apostolic Penitentiary. One must furthermore mention the great contribution he made through his frequent and constructive participation in the preparatory work for the Second Vatican Council and during the sittings of the Council itself.

When certain people, emphasizing various difficulties, objected to the use of Latin in the Council and raised the possibility of allowing the use of the various modern languages coupled with a system of simultaneous translation, His Eminence replied, first of all, that "to celebrate an ecumenical council with everyone speaking in different modern languages with a system of cubicles and headphones would give the impression, if not of the repudiation, at least of the demotion of the official language of the Church, and that by act of the Church herself and at a moment in which some parties are looking to diminish or even abandon the use of such a language." The Cardinal said that one would not need to speak in Classical Latin; it would suffice to use that unadorned, fluid, flexible but correct Latin in use in the departments of the Roman Curia or that spoken in the advanced ecclesiastical schools. As for the conciliar acts the Cardinal was of the opinion that they should be composed in the "noble tradition of Classical Latin".

After a long illness, Cardinal Bacci passed away in his apartment at the Vatican on the morning of January 20, 1971. On the evening before, Pope Paul VI had visited him as he lay dying.

---

1 The first edition appeared under the title *Varia latinitatis scripta: inscriptiones orationes epistulae eorumque lexicon vocabulorum quae difficilius latine redduntur*, [in Civitate Vaticana], Typis polyglottis Vaticanis, 1944. It was afterwards divided into two volumes: *Varia latinitatis scripta. I: Lexicon vocabulorum quae difficilius latine redduntur*, Rome, Societas libraria "Studium", 1963. II: *Inscriptiones orationes epistulae*, Rome, Societas libraria "Studium", 1955.

ANTONIO CARDINAL BACCI

The body was prepared and exposed in the entrance hall of the Cardinal's apartment on the third floor of the Museo Lapidario. The Funeral Mass took place in St. Peter's Basilica; the celebrant was Peter Canisius van Lierde, the Pope's Vicar General for Vatican City. The last *commendatio et valedictio* was given, at the Pope's request, by Fernando Cardinal Cento. The body was then taken to Florence and thence to the church in Giugnola where it was buried.

FLORENTINE MEMORIES

Another funeral was celebrated in Florence in Santa Maria del Fiore on January 24, 1971 with Ermenegildo Cardinal Florit, Archbishop of Florence, presiding. The burial took place that afternoon in Giugnola in the presence of Monsignor Antonio Ravagli, Auxiliary Bishop of Florence.

Here is the Latin epitaph composed in his memory:

ANTONIVS · BACCI
S · R · E · CARDINALIS · DIACONVS · TIT · S · EVGENII
DIE · VIGESIMA · IANVARII · A · MDCCCCLXXI
AETATIS · SVAE · LXXXV
CORPVS · GRAVI · MORBO · CORRVPTVM
IN · TERRIS · RELIQVIT
IPSE · VERO · AD · SERENA · DEI · TEMPLA
LAETVS · MIGRAVIT
LATINITATIS · CVLTOR · ET · AMATOR · IN · PRIMIS
QVATTVOR · ROMANORVM · PONTIFICVM
LATINA · VOX · EXSTITIT
EORVMQVE · PRAECEPTA · NITIDE · ORNAVIT
EX · HVMILI · POTENS · FACTVS
NON · NOMINE · SED · VIRTVTE · CONFISVS
MODESTIAM · VITAE · VSQVE · RETINVIT
VIR · PIETATIS · INSIGNIS
QVOD · INCONCVSSA · FIDE · CREDIDIT
HOC · NVNC · VIDET.

* * *

ANTONIO BACCI
CARDINAL DEACON OF THE HOLY ROMAN CHURCH
OF THE TITLE OF ST. EUGENIUS

Antonio Cardinal Bacci
DIED ON JANUARY 20, 1971 AT EIGHTY-FIVE YEARS OF AGE
HE LEFT BEHIND A BODY DESTROYED BY MORTAL ILLNESS
AND HAPPILY MOVED TO THE HOME OF GOD ALMIGHTY
PREEMINENT STUDENT AND LOVER OF LATIN
HE WAS THE LATIN VOICE OF FOUR ROMAN PONTIFFS
WHOSE TEACHINGS HE ADORNED WITH ELOQUENCE
FROM HUMBLE BEGINNINGS HE ROSE TO BECOME GREAT
THROUGH HIS ABILITY NOT MERELY ON ACCOUNT OF HIS NAME
HE REMAINED MODEST
HE WAS A MAN NOTEWORTHY FOR HIS PIETY
WHAT HE BELIEVED WITH AN UNSHAKING FAITH
THAT HE NOW SEES

At the request of the Cardinal Archbishop, one of his students, Msgr. Giulio Lorini, pronounced the funeral elegy in the cathedral. Here is an extract:

> The newspapers both in Rome and in Florence have already spoken of His Eminence Cardinal Bacci. They called him a famous Latinist, a man of deep piety, the man whose *Meditations* were used by Pope John. Our Archbishop characterized him as "a most worthy son of the Church of Florence". The Holy Father calls him "a noble figure of the good and faithful servant of the Lord and of the Church who performed his long service with self-denial and zeal for the Holy See".... As a young man he went down to the seminary of Firenzuola from Giugnola, a village in the mountains on the border with the Romagna.... Very quickly that boy, as his first instructor Don Trentanove relates, went to the top of the class. "The boys from the mountains — Bacci himself used to say — have a genius like a wedge; they penetrate slowly, but they go deep." And so in those golden years of the seminary of Firenzuola he was able to make advanced studies and even earn his degree in Dogmatic Theology at the *Collegio Teologico Fiorentino*. In 1909 he was ordained priest, but his vow of obedience kept him at the seminary for another nine years as a well-loved professor, esteemed by the students.... Early in the morning he used to go up to the churches scattered

over the mountains to celebrate Mass, hear confessions, and preach along with the parish priests. His youth as a priest bore fruit in a volume of poetry published at that time, *Oasi: Rime e Ritmi Giovanili*. Cardinal Mistrangelo sent him down to Florence to the Major Seminary as superior and instructor. He arrived at the villa of Lecceto where he found a small group of seminarians reduced in numbers by the war of 1915–1918 and whom not even the venerated father figure of the Rector was succeeding in keeping calm. He was warmly greeted and became at once the friend of Maestro Francesco Bagnoli who, having gone up there for a few days of vacation, entertained us with some of his compositions, among which was *Dolce Signora*, based on a text by Bacci himself.

So passed a couple of years. One morning after the usual walk on the grounds of the villa, Cardinal Mistrangelo, taking leave of him with thanks, added, "Bacci, come to see me in half an hour."

He was very happy, mistakenly thinking of his mother and his sisters Bettina and Agnese and of a church he had always dreamed of. He went to the Cardinal and returned rather dejected. The reason why became clear in November. He was called to Rome to be a *minutante* at the Secretariat of State. With tears in his eyes he gave the news to the old rector in the refectory, but the students to whom he had become a brother and to whom he had given his clear lectures were also disappointed....

For ten years he was the teacher of Italian and French in the seminary at Firenzuola and for two years more in that at Florence. He made a serious study of Latin in Rome, and his friend Msgr. Giulio Bonardi searched in the library for works of our sixteenth century Latinists and sent them to him in Rome. With intelligence and love he studied this language "alive," as he wrote, "vital, and essential for every cultured person".... It should therefore not come as a surprise that he made such a great defense of this "official language of the Church, *sacrum latinum*." His career (if one may use that word) advanced rapidly.

In 1931 he was named Secretary of Briefs to Princes, the man who had to compose the principal and most important documents of the Holy See in his "clear Latin", as Pius XI used to call it.

It is hard to find him photographed in the solemn ceremonies in the Vatican; perhaps he preferred to stay in the open air near his apartment in the Vatican Gardens, where every evening he took a walk, at first with his friend Fr. Cordovani and then with Fr. Ciappi, another one of his friends, who loyally helped him to the very end. He once told me, "The whole of that encyclical passed under my nails," and he truly felt the grave duty of composing in Latin the documents that would bring the thinking of the Church to the whole world, a responsibility that weighed on his conscience. He was aware of a certain uneasiness with regard to his own health, which was always a bit delicate.... When he had passed his sixties, he asked Pius XII to be relieved of his duties and to be allowed to return to his mountains, but the Pope wanted him nearby; even during the summer holiday Pius XII did not want him to go too far away so he could recall him to Rome if necessary. "The Pope won't let me go," he said, and then sought to console himself by writing that perhaps naïve book *Candele che si spengono* as a sort of nostalgic return into his long gone youth.... He was always glad to visit his people in Giugnola; he would go back to Santa Cristina in the Val di Pesa and stay with his nephew Don Francesco... all the while conducting himself on those occasions with that Franciscan simplicity that is not unbecoming to the sacred purple but renders it even more attractive.

He returned to Giugnola for the last time on the sixtieth anniversary of his ordination. No one was invited except two priests, his old fellow students who, without saying anything, came there. He took them into the little garden of the family house and brought them for a visit to the family chapel dedicated to St. Anthony where his tomb had already been prepared. Then, seven months and five days later, as Fr. Ciappi relates, after a painful agony, lovingly assisted and consoled by his most dear devotion to the Virgin Mary,... he returned to Giugnola to rest eternally, truly blessed because *"Video quod credidi"*, as he had written on his tomb, blessed in the vision of God.

11

The Latinity of Antonio Cardinal Bacci

CONTRADICTIONS AND OPPORTUNITIES

by Carlo Nardi

I gladly take this opportunity to present some ideas, however tentative, about Antonio Cardinal Bacci and Latin composition. I will extend my analysis and digress into some further considerations on the use of Latin.

TAKING UP A PROPOSAL

Should I say something about whether writing in Latin even makes sense? Why not? It would only be to illustrate my conviction: one may write in Latin so long as it is really Latin prose or poetry in the manner of the solemn discourse of Cardinal Bacci. But the discourse is really Latin only on condition that, if not thought directly and spontaneously in Latin like the lyric poetry of Pascoli or the teaching of Leo XIII, it must be at least rethought in Latin.[1]

There is one further condition, namely, that one enjoys writing in Latin. To be sure, writing in Latin is usually an activity secondary to expressing oneself in one's own language, but it pays off if one's closest and, I would say, dearest associates have written or write in Latin so that the joy of a real dialogue leads one to think or at least to rethink in Latin.

Now this is not obvious. In fact, two acute Latin experts on translation deserve a hearing, Cicero, an author in the true

---

[1] A. Traina and E. Mandruzzato, *Giovanni Pascoli, Poemi cristiani*, Testo latino a fronte, second edition, Rizzoli, Milan, 2004; cfr. A Traina and P. Ferratini, *Storie di Roma*, Testo latino a fronte, Rizzoli, Milan, 1994.

sense of the word *auctor* and, therefore, an ideal model of good Latin prose, and St. Jerome, whom legend and sacred art have represented with the stern discipline of the scholar, capable of taming the passions of a lion; his asceticism was consecrated to the equally passionate love of doctrine in devotion to the Church in its Roman headquarters, as the neglected but present red hat suggests. The greatest expression of Jerome's professional passion was to translate and to write commentaries for the purpose of interpreting Sacred Scripture. The letter in the form of a treatise, *De optimo genere interpretandi*, is his methodological legacy; for him, to interpret is to be faithful not to the word in its literal sense but to the word's meaning, thought, and possibly image that is present in the original language and needs to be rethought, felt, and expressed in different words in the other language, in his case in Latin.[2]

FROM RECENT HISTORY

This essay has its roots in the context of my Florentine education, which I received from the Faculty of Letters where, around the middle of the twentieth century, Ugo Enrico Paoli was publishing his *Scriver latino*, still a useful supplement to detailed grammars and accurate dictionaries.[3] I was introduced to this masterpiece by my dear teacher Nilo Casini when I was a high school student at the Liceo Dante; he was the same Casini who was coauthor with Paoli of the *Index emendatae latinitatis*.[4]

The preference to write in Latin correctly and well (not only *emendate* but fully *latine*) in an almost exclusively Ciceronian style is found in the ecclesiastical education of our

---

[2] C. Nardi, *Ancora in compagnia di Girolamo, Note sull'ambiente, i criteri e la fortuna della Vulgata*, Vivens homo, 4 (1993) 127-161; C. Moreschini, R. Palla, *San Girolamo, Lettere: Introduzione di C. M., Traduzione di R. P., Testo latino a fronte*, Rizzoli, Milano, 2000. Cfr. A. Penna, *Girolamo, dottore della Chiesa, santo*, in Biblioteca sanctorum, VI, Città Nuova, Roma, 1965, columns 1109-1103.
[3] *Scriver latino, Guida a comporre e tradurre in lingua latina*, Principato, Milan and Messina, 1952.
[4] Le Monnier, Florence, 1967.

The Latinity of Antonio Cardinal Bacci

seminarians at the three local colleges, the Eugenianum, La Calza e Cestello, and Firenzuola; the third of these is an institution without which one cannot understand the elegant Latin prose of Cardinal Bacci. In this connection we may mention two scholars, from the secular clergy the metropolitan canon, professor at the theological college Emilio Sanesi, and from the Piarist tradition Fr. Ermenegildo Pistelli, whose name cannot fail to remind one of the Latin work of Pascoli, of which he was the editor.[5]

In short, I admit that from my youth I have received an inheritance in the Ciceronian tradition that I have tried to cultivate—I know not how successfully—when I composed the exercises of my high-school years as well as an occasional short article in *Latinitas, Prometheus,* and *Vivens homo,* not to mention the plaque commemorating the dedication of the parish church of the Ascension in Florence at the welcome request of Don Giuseppe Padovani. For this I owe thanks to my teachers like Nilo Casini and indirectly to a whole tradition of thought, taste, and sensitivity.

In the environment of the *Istituto di Studi Superiori* and, from 1924, in the University of Florence, skill in writing in Latin, in elegant Latin, was certainly coupled with the rigorous transalpine attention to philology of the end of the nineteenth century, particularly in Germany; the methods of Ulrich von Wilamowitz are to be found and bear fruit in Domenico Comparetti, Girolamo Vitelli, and Giorgio Pasquali.[6] However, in the Florentine ecclesiastical environment, under suspicion during the modernist crisis with its painful episode of Don Salvatore Minocchi, the cult of Latin seems to have

---

[5] *Studia humanitatis nella Facoltà Teologica dell'Italia centrale,* Tra filologia e cristologia, in G. Canobbio and S. Nocetti [editors] *Studi in onore di Don Severino Dianich, EDB,* Bologna (to appear soon).

[6] Cf. G. Pasquali, *Pagine stravaganti: Introduzione di G. Pugliese Carratelli. I. Pagine stravaganti vecchie e nuove. Pagine meno stravaganti, II: Terze pagine stravaganti. Stravaganze quarte e supreme,* Sansoni, Florence, 1968; P. Treves, *Lo studio dell'antichità classica nell'Ottocento, (La letteratura italiana, Storia e testi 72),* Ricciardi, Milan and Naples, 1962, pages 1052-1103, 1113-1126.

been part of a nostalgic return to pure scholarship.[7] These are the origins of the courtly if not pompous features recognizable in the stylistic plan of Cardinal Bacci, who was soon after summoned to go from Florence to the Vatican for a positon at the Apostolic See with international responsibilities, namely, the correspondence with *principes*, that is, with heads of state.

CARDINAL BACCI'S LEXICON

What was intended by the program of Cardinal Bacci, the intention expressed in the *Lexicon* in August of that sad year 1944? The *Lexicon* was included in the volume *Varia latinitatis scripta, Inscriptiones orationes epistulae eorumque Lexicon vocabulorum quae difficilius latine redduntur, Antonii Bacci ab epistulis Pont. Max. ad principes, Typis polyglottis Vaticanis, in Civitate Vaticana, 1944*. This was the full name if the work, as we read on the title page of a copy previously owned by Ermenegildo Cardinal Florit that was donated to the *Studio Teologico Fiorentino*. The *Lexicon* offers expressions, most often Ciceronian, whose purpose is to express in Latin, in the best Latin, Italian idioms found in current Italian usage. These include Italian idioms, mostly legal, that have become part of the technical language, and new words and phrases required in the wake of scientific advances.

The attempt of Cardinal Bacci goes beyond the goal proposed, for example, by the gymnasium text Campanini-Carboni[8] or the high-school text Badellino,[9] or the most recent *Dizionario di Italiano-Latino* of Gian Biagio Conte, Emilio Pianezzola and Giuliano Ranucci. This last work is intended to be an "aid to learn the Latin names of ancient things, not of

---

7   Cf. S. Minocchi, *Memorie di un modernista, a cura di A. Agnoletto*, Vallecchi, Florence, 1974. Cfr. M. Tagliaferri, *L'Unità Cattolica, Studio di una mentalità*. Università Gregoriana, Rome, 1993.
8   G. Campanini and G. Carboni, *Vocabolario latino-italiano italiano-latino*, Edizione riveduta e ampliata da B. G. Bertazzoli e C. Piazzino, Paravia, Torino, 1961.
9   O. Badellino, *Dizionario italiano-latino*, Rosemberg & Sellier, Torino, 1962 (first edition), 1965 (second edition).

modern things ... without technical terms or modern objects or concepts".[10]

Bacci's book, with its wealth of Latin equivalents and its specific Latinisms, has the sense, style, and spirit of Latin prose. It is necessary to keep this in mind if one wants to translate into Latin effectively or at least to transfer a concept or perhaps an image from one language to another, in this case from Italian to Latin, in exact accordance with the rules of the great Latin theoreticians of translation, the aforementioned Cicero and St. Jerome.

Bacci gave special attention to those Italian terms or expressions whose literal translations into Latin do not give the true meaning or even make no sense at all, proposing instead ones that better render the Italian word or phrase. Paoli and Casini, in their above-mentioned *Index*, indicate with didactic clarity words that can be easily misunderstood because they are apparent homonymns in the ancestral and derivative languages; for example, the Italian verb *ottenere* is to be rendered in Latin by *consequi* or *adipisci*, while *obtinere* in Latin means simply *tenere* in Italian. Bacci anticipates them to the point of "emending" in a Ciceronian sense Latin expressions that entered into use from scholastic, legal, or, at times tastefully, liturgical Latin.

PERPLEXITY

Now, in this respect, when he "corrects" *in hac lacrimarum valle* with *in hac vita aerumnorum plena* (page 319), he seems to have succumbed to an excess of Ciceronianism. And that is what I meant by courtly pomposity.

In effect, the Latinity of Cardinal Bacci follows an exclusively Ciceronian stile and as a result revives the debates in the recurrent controversies in the sphere of humanism and among the lovers of *humanae* and *bonae litterae* in general. There comes to mind the argument between the versatile

---

10 Le Monnier-L'Espresso Repubblica, Firenze-Roma, 2004, 6.

Politian and the Ciceronian Paolo Cortesi and in 1512 that between Giovan Francesco Pico (a follower of Savonarola) and Cardinal Pietro Bembo.[11]

There is also the ironic Erasmus who, in his *Ciceronianus sive de optimo dicendi genere*, somewhat causticly criticized those Latinists who paganized for the love of Cicero and who, convinced that they were disfiguring their classical Latin prose by using the names Christ and Mary, translated (if one can call it that) those appellations by *Jove* and *Diana*.[12]

It is most likely that the paganizers just mentioned were from the environment of the Roman Curia. After all, Cortesi would become the author of *De cardinalatu*[13] and Bembo went on to be honored with the Roman purple. Ciceronianism would be adopted to the bitter end by the *ratio studiorum* of the Jesuits, for whom *stylus ex uno fere Cicerone sumendus est*.[14]

In the times of Urban VIII an excess of classicism led to the correction of the liturgical hymns in the Roman Breviary: *Accessit latinitas, recessit pietas*. More recently, the philological restoration of the supposed original in the revised *Liturgia horarum* was not to the benefit of euphony, and anyway

---

11 Angelo Poliziano, Paolo Cortesio, and Paolo Cortesi, Angelo Poliziano, in E. Garin, *Prosatori latini del Quattrocento* (La letteratura italiana, Studi e testi 13), Ricciardi, Milan and Naples, 1952, pages 902-904 and 904 -910; G. Santangelo, *Le epistole "De immitatione" di Giovanfrancesco Pico della Mirandola e di Pietro Bembo*, Olschki, Florence, 1954; cf. G. Santangelo, *La polemica fra Pietro Bembo e Gian Francesco Pico interno al principio d'imitazione*, "Rinascimento" I (1950) 323-339. Cf. A. Sabbadini, *Storia del ciceronianesimo e di altre questioni letterarie nell'età della Rinascenza*, Loescher, Turin, 1885; C. Nardi, *Una pagina "umanistica" di Teodoreto di Ciro e un'interpretazione di Zanobi Acciaiuoli*, "Atti e Memorie dell'Accademia Toscana di Scienze e Lettere 'La Colombaria'", 56 (1991) 9-63; M. Fumaroli, *L'età dell'eloquenza, Retorica e "res literaria" del Rinascimento alle soglie dell'epoca classica*, Adelphi, Milan, 2002.
12 A. Gambaro, *Desiderio Erasmo da Rotterdam. Il Ciceroniano o dello stile migliore. Testo latino critico, traduzione italiana, prefazione, introduzione e note*, La Scuola, Brescia, 1965.
13 R. Ricciardi, *Cortesi, Paolo*, in *Dizionario biografico degli italiani*, XIX, Treccani, Rome, 1983, 766-770.
14 *Regulae professoris rhetoricae* 1, in A. Bianchi, *Ratio et institutio studiorum Societatis Iesu, Introduzione e traduzione. Testo latino a fronte*, Rizzoli, Milan, 2002, 264.

divine worship must not be made to submit to philological criteria—the intention of the Council was the elimination of whatever smacked of mythology[15]—for the liturgy has the sacrosanct right to preserve, as well as to remove, successive stratifications.

TOWARDS A LIVING LATIN

Any choice of Bacci's smacking of paganism would have aroused the perplexity of Erasmus. The Cardinal holds his nose in the case of *Salvator* in order to designate Jesus with a non-classical term. He also keeps his distance even from St. Augustine, although the latter is expressly cited by him (page 404) to vindicate the novelty and linguistic legitimacy of that word *Salvator* that Christian usage had made Latin.[16] After all, the pastoral choice *melius est reprehendant grammatici quam non intellegant populi* ("it is better that the grammarians disapprove than that the people not understand") is characteristic of St. Augustine, because the Gospel must be preached and understood.[17] The same Augustine preferred the Biblical "humility" of the Hebraizing and Hellenizing versions of Scripture[18]—with their "smooth and soft" style adopted by catechesis and patristic homiletics—to the fascinating eloquence of Cicero (*Tulliana dignitas*).

One cannot doubt the vitality, originality, and variety of patristic and then mediaeval, monastic, and Carolingian Latin, expressive of the *amour des lettres* and of the desire for God, elegant and devout, so dear to Fr. Jean Leclerq.[19] Latin too is the rigorous *stilus parisiensis* of the school, by means of which the humanists place themselves in a multiform dialectic with one another in a Latin just as varied as there were humanists

---

15   *Constitutio de sacra liturgia "Sacrosanctum Consilium"* 93, in *Enchiridion Vaticanum*, I, EDB, Bologna, 1976 (first edition), n. 165, 72.
16   *Sermo* 299, 6.
17   *Enarrationes in Psalmos* 138, 20, in Ps. 138, 15.
18   *Confessiones* III, 5, 9.
19   *Cultura umanistica e desiderio di Dio. Studio sulla letteratura monastica del Medio Evo*, Prefazione di C. Leonardi. Sansoni, Florence, 1983.

themselves, with their multiple theories on the imitation of the classic authors, from the rigorous Ciceronianism of the orations to the noble style of a single dialogue, the only one to incorporate the clearly freer Cicero of the epistles.

In fact, between unhistorical and perhaps inappropriate Ciceronianism and a Latin that is a literal reproduction of a trend of a modern language and therefore smacks of the artificial, the sloppy, and, ultimately, the dead, there is room for a whole range of equally Latin styles, from an eloquence that copies that of Cicero to a mode of expression that brings with it the freedom and the joy of entering into dialogue with other authors, those of the so called silver, or late, or mediaeval, or humanistic age.

Now there is also the Latin of Seneca, Tacitus, and Apuleius, just as there is that of the Christians; each has its own style, the style that is the man and the thing at the same time, as Buffon has said. There is the Latin of the nervous, concrete and conceptual Tertullian, that of the staid Cyprian, Lactantius, and Leo, and the most original Latin of Augustine and Jerome.[20] Why deprive oneself, even in writing, of their company? Why not pass from an exclusive Ciceronianism to an intensely apostolic colloquialism, cordially spiritual, doctrinally committed, authoritatively dignified, the expression of a more jagged and living humanity to be led to Christ?

On the other hand, there is also the Cicero of the epistles, who talks and writes with his heart in his hand, so Ciceronianism risks pursuing a Latin more Ciceronian than that of Cicero himself that even worse than being contradictory borders on the ridiculous. Even more, a hyperciceronianism risks dissolving into the primacy of vocabulary; to the irony of Erasmus there appears to be added that of Giuseppe Gioachino Belli,

---

20 Cf. Chr. Mohrmann, *Études sur le latin des chrétiens*, I–III, Edizioni di Storia e Letteratura, Rome, 1961–1965; H. Hagendahl, *Cristianesimo latino e cultura classica. Da Tertulliano a Cassiodoro*. Introduzione di P. Siniscalco, Borla, Rome, 1988. Cf. C. Nardi, *Fra storia e teologia*. Prefazione di G. Ravasi, in Leone Magno, Sermoni. I: Introduzione. Nardini, Florence, 1997, 101–119.

with his "little marquis Eufemio" and "the knight on the armchair", "researching in Calepino's Dictionary whether *Ancona* is written with or without an *h*".

BUT LATIN RETHOUGHT IN LATIN

Ciceronianism, involving as it does the risk of pursuing a crystallized Latin, would seem to be very unwelcoming to neologisms, on the creation of which, however, Cardinal Bacci lavished his attention. Whether we accept a technical term that the modern languages have coined for the most part from Greek, a term that nothing prevents being transferred into Latin, maybe with a warning by means of *qui dicitur* or *ut aiunt* that reduces somewhat the ugliness of the artificial concoction, or whether one is attempting a Latin translation on the basis of analogy with some object or concept, one of the *realia* or entities of reason, known and given a name by someone who wrote in Latin, in both cases one does not reproduce Cicero but one expresses oneself somewhat differently. The point is that that something else must be Latin, that is to say, the fruit of thinking and feeling in Latin, in spirit and in letter, one might say in body and soul.

Contradictions seem to me to arise from a narrowly applied Ciceronianism. Bacci's discussion with respect to *servator* and *salvator* is symptomatic of this. The *Tulliana dignitas* of which St. Augustine spoke while always keeping a proper distance but which Cardinal Bacci defended in, I would say, an absolute way, seems an aspect of an abnormal exaggeration of the dignity of the cardinalate and indirectly of the papacy, especially in the period between the two Vatican councils,[21] to which some-

---

21 R. Aubert, *I progressi dell'ultramontanismo*, in R. Aubert and G. Martina (editors) *Il pontificato di Pio IX (1846-1878)*, I, in A. Fliche and V. Martin (editors) *Storia della Chiesa*. XXI, I, Paoline, Cinisello Balsamo, (Milan) 1990 (fourth edition), 409-476; R. Aubert, Il Concilio Vaticano I, in R. Aubert and G. Martina (editors) *Il pontificato di Pio IX (1846-1878)*, I, in A, Fliche and V. Martin (editors) *Storia della Chiesa*. XXI. II. Paoline, Cinisello Balsamo, (Milan) 1990 (fourth edition), 477-561; A. Zambarbieri, *La devozione al papa*, in E. Guerriero and A. Zambarbieri (editors) *La Chiesa e la società industriale (1878-1922)*, II, in A.

thing more polished and sublime would have been suited than linguistic considerations not only Augustinian but Patristic in general and on the whole humanistic.

However, if one wants to write a sentence in Latin, if it was not thought originally in that language (as was the case of the almost perfect bilingualism of Pascoli or Pope Pecci), the sentence has to be rethought in Latin before taking the pen in hand, or the pen itself must be repeatedly taken in hand for that *labor limae* that Horace recommended.[22] Otherwise, the resulting slovenliness is a sign of disrespect for those who have thought, loved, felt, and lived in that language on a high level or at least on a human level, from the speeches of Cicero to the graffiti on the walls of Pompeii. In this sense reading Cardinal Bacci is more than beneficial, especially for whoever performs chancery duties *ab epistulis*, because encyclical letters, and whatever else for that matter, must be written well. Such was the attitude of Coluccio Salutati with respect to the affairs of the Commune of the Florentine Republic as well as, obviously, that of the Roman Chancellery itself. Francesco Di Capua's essays have much to say on this subject.[23]

A LANGUAGE UNIVERSALLY ACCEPTABLE

I think that writing well in Latin is a duty that is worth the trouble of acquiring, especially by a cardinal, who, as a clergyman of Rome, has his dignity in the service of advice to and collaboration with the Petrine ministry of the Roman Pontiff; a cardinal must be conscious of that universality in accordance with which Latin can still offer a means of impartial

---

Fliche and V. Martin (editors) *Storia della Chiesa*. XXII. II, 1992 (second edition), 9–81. Cf. D. Menozzi, *La Chiesa cattolica e la secolarizzazione*, Einaudi, Turin, 1993; P. De Marco, *Modernità di Roma. Per un saggio sulla forma cattolica*, in "Vivens homo", 481–508. Also: A. Cortesi (ed.) 1904–2004: Yves Congar, *Un maestro da ricordare, un servizio teologico da continuare*, in "Rivista di ascetica e mistica", 74 (2005) 1–303.

22 *Epistulae* II, 3: *ars poëtica* 290–291.

23 *Il ritmo prosaico nelle lettere dei papi e nei documenti della cancelleria romana dal IV al XIV secolo*, I–III. Lateranum, Rome, 1937, 1939, 1946, and *Fonti ed esempi per lo studio dello 'stylus curiae Romanae'*, Maglione, Rome, 1941.

communication and be a useful and humble antidote, today more than ever, to the arrogance of nations, especially when one of them claims a universality that does not belong to it—exclusive leadership, so to speak, of the world community—because that belongs to humanity as a whole.[24]

Certainly if Latin is the obvious inheritance of the hegemony of that City that imagined itself to be identical with the world, as the pagan Rutilio Namaziano melancholically observed at the eventful beginning of the fifth century,[25] it is also the language that gave literacy to the conquered as well as the conquerors. The solemn accusatory words against all imperialism on the lips of the Caledonian Calgacus are Latin: *ubi solitudinem faciunt, pacem appellant*.[26] The account of the trial of the martyrs of Scilla in Numidia, poor, common people, summoned before the Roman magistrate and executed on July 17, 180, makes their words resound, Latin words, in a Latin old and at the same time new, customary Latin, not the exclusive jargon of a secret sect, but new because expressive of Christianity as the new life and therefore noble more than ever.[27]

On the other hand, cardinals have given us an example of a Latin that is devotedly Christian, pastorally Catholic, loftily elegant, freely Ciceronian, tastefully patristic, piously

---

24 John XXIII, *Constitutio apostolica "Veterum sapientia"(February 22, 1962)*, "Acta Apostolicae Sedis" 54 (1962) 130: "lingua Latina ad provehendum apud populos quoslibet omnem humanitatis cultum est peraccommodata: cum invidiam non commoveat, singulis gentibus se aequabilem praestet, nullius partibus faveat, omnibus postremo sit grata et amica": cf. 129-135. Cf. K. Rahner, *Il latino lingua della Chiesa*, Paideia, Brescia, 1964; A. Drigani, *Diritto canonico, lingua Latina e teologia. Osservazioni sul decreto* Novo codice. "Vivens homo" 14 (2003) 165-171. cf. 171-175.
25 *De reditu suo*, I 66.
26 Tacitus, *De vita et moribus Iulii Agricolae* 30, 7: cf. 29, 4-33, I. Cf. R. Tosi, *Dizionario delle sentenze latine e greche*, Rizzoli, Milan, 1993, n. 1209, 546-547.
27 *Acta martyrum Scilitanorum*, in A. A. A. Bastianensen et al., *Atti e passioni dei martiri*, Mondadori, Milan, 1996, 97-105. Cf. *Epistula ad Diognetum*, 5, 1; cf. 5, 1-6, 10; K. Promm, *Il cristianesimo come novità di vita, Il cristianesimo di fronte al mondo pagano*, Italian edition edited by P. Rossano, Morcelliana, Brescia, 1955; C. Nardi, *Patristica e laicità, Rileggendo la Lettera a Diogneto*, "Nicolaus" 20 (1993), fasc. 2, 105-151.

humanistic; it is the *Catechism* of the Council of Trent, that *Catechismus Romanus ad Parochos*, the fruit of the work of cardinals of the Reformation and Counter Reformation periods, the reading of which is an edifying experience[28] since it realizes that ideal of "noble simplicity" that the Second Vatican Council prescribes for a liturgical context, especially for the Latin rite.[29]

---

28 P. Rodriguez, I. Adeva, R. Lanzetti, and M. Merino, *Catechismus Romanus seu Catechismus ex decreto Concilii Tridentini ad Parochos Pii Quinti Pont. Max. iussu editus*, Libreria Editrice Vaticana – Ediciones Universidad de Navarra, Città del Vaticano, Barcelona, and Pamplona, 1989.
29 *Constitutio de sacra liturgia "Sacrosanctum Concilium"*, 34, in *Enchiridion Vaticanum*, I, EDB, Bologna, 1976 (tenth edition), n. 55, p. 40.

III

The Works of Antonio Cardinal Bacci
by Pier Carlo Tagliaferri

ANTONIO CARDINAL BACCI (1885-1971), famous Latinist, owed much of his prestige and fame to the environment which, in the years of his youth, provided for his education and his spiritual and cultural training. In fact, he attended the seminary of Firenzuola throughout his high school years, where, at the express wish and desire of the founder, teachers of the first class were invited to teach literary and scientific subjects. This establishment was opened in 1801 by the Archbishop of Florence, Antonio Martini, who was famous for his translation of the Old and New Testaments. It was destined to receive youths with a vocation to the priesthood, and the Archbishop summoned to the faculty men of great reputation and of solid and specific training and education, among whom one may note Raffaello Del Ghio, the collaborator of Abbot Manuzi in the revision and correction for the reprinting of the *Vocabolario della Lingua Italiana*, and Raffaello Caverni, who, "during the ten years that he spent there as teacher, taught philosophy and dogma and established the school of physics and of the natural sciences". Lorenzo Mancini, who was later lecturer at the University of Pisa, also taught there. In that environment ever open and in communication with the outside world (for even students without vocations were regularly admitted), a literary academy came into being with end-of-the-year essays and literary entertainments of undoubted quality, so much so as to receive the applause of Luigi Venturi and of Niccolò Tommaseo. There was also founded as evidence of the seriousness and liveliness of the academic program the so-called *Accademia dei Ravvivati*, which had a stimulating effect, aimed at encouraging the most brilliant and creative intellects among the young guests. The "poetic exercises" in imitation of Catullus, Horace, and Vergil were frequent, and beyond their artistic value, they demonstrated a considerable theoretical command of the Latin language on the part of the student authors. Theatrical enterprises were constantly put on the stage, and the education in music and chant was intense. In this connection it is well to recall that in 1893 Lorenzo Perosi arrived in nearby Imola. In the "Stoppani" Tower and in its basement there was installed—it was inaugurated on July 17, 1881 with the extraordinary participation of Abbot Antonio Stoppani—the meteorological and seismological observatory, whose data were constantly being forwarded to the Ximenes Observatory of the Piarist fathers in Florence. In addition, the Salvi Library (so called from the name of Salvi Bonaccorsi, who gave the seminary more than 3,000 books) had at its disposal a literary patrimony of around 7,000 published items ("and that is without counting the miscellaneous items, the journals, and the uncatalogued books," as Stefano Casini affirmed in his *Dizionario*, sent to the press in 1914). In conclusion, one may truly say that at Firenzuola *florebat olim studium*. And from this environment, so stimulating in both the human and spiritual aspect, truly pregnant with culture, Antonio Bacci was able to accomplish his education and have his personal gifts and potential developed. In his seminary, when his time as student was over, he stayed longer in the capacity of teacher and superior.

The *Cardinél*, as his fellow townsmen of Giugnola and Piancaldoli used to call him affectionately in their harmonious Emilian dialect, is most of all known as a man of great classical culture and of profound knowledge of the Latin language. Nevertheless, it adds to his merit that on November 6, 1910 he took part as founding member in the meeting that formed the *Cassa Rurale di Prestiti e di Risparmio di Piancaldoli*, the Rural Savings and Loan Association of Piancaldoli, demonstrating in this way that in times of usury (a horrible offense quite common "in those days" to the harm of people least able to defend themselves, especially the poorest and men and women of low birth laboring in agriculture) he had close to heart, not only the cultivation of literary studies but also solidarity with society as a whole.

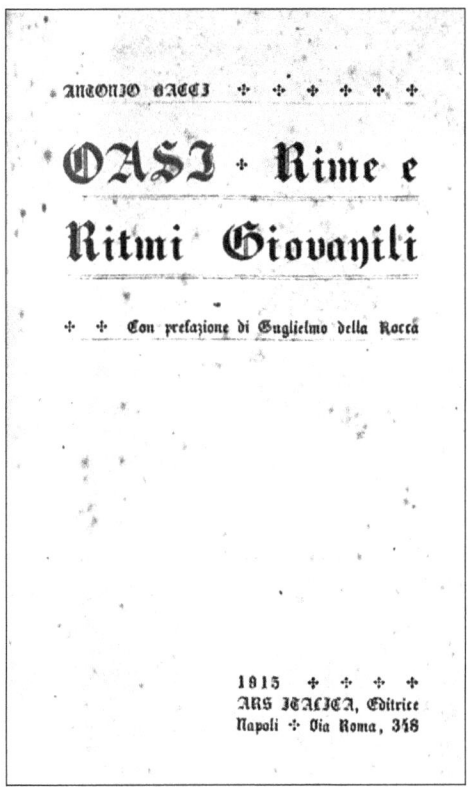

Oasi: Rime e Ritmi giovanili
ARS ITALICA EDIT., NAPLES, 1915

IN 1915 THE NEAPOLITAN PUBLISHING HOUSE *ARS Italica* put out the volume *Oasi: Rime e Ritmi giovanili* (*Oasis: Youthful Rhymes and Rhythms*), which was dedicated "to the dear memory of Don Giuseppe Benelli", teacher of literature and philosophy at the seminary of Firenzuola and also at the same time rector.

In the preface to this publication, the future cardinal "shows himself to be"—so Guglielmo della Rocca writes—"a natural born poet, and his undamaged soul, whole and communicative, captures suddenly and without shadow the virgin beauties of creation, the soul of humble realities, the beauty of small scenes."

In the *Dizionario biografico geografico storico del Comune di Firenzuola (Biographical, Geogrphical, and Historical Dictionary of the Town of Firenzuola)*, Stefano Casini had this to say about the first publication of Don Bacci:

> The new Vice Rector of our Seminary, where good studies flourish, ... is Don Antonio Bacci from Piancaldoli. He has recently given proof of his good education by publishing a book of rhymes and rhythms that shows him to be of the stuff of original poet and good cultivator of letters. We can therefore predict that he has a secure future in literature if he continues his work to improve in this art.... Bacci's muse is also pleasing because for the most part it is a country muse. In the poem *Eroe (Hero)* he describes the life of our mountain curate. In the *Rime* one sees again the black shadows of the old castles on the green slopes of our Santerno. In the *Battitura dei Castagni*, he recounts our beautiful way of life in October.

Even *Civiltà Cattolica*, the authoritative magazine of the Jesuits, printed a long review of this publication, writing, among other things:

> In this young man we like the boldness of the soul that rises far from the bursting little waterfalls of certain poetizing youngsters, imitators of the idols of fashion. We like the clarity of the style, although it is not yet perfect. But most of all we like the beautiful and cordial frankness with which he sings his Christian ideal in the face of the literary and non-literary world.[1]

We present some of the poems below:

---

[1] Quad. 1567, October 2, 1915

L'EROE

*Fiocca in ridda la neve i suoi misteri
bianchi, tessendo enigmi ad ogni ramo,
nel cinereo silenzio sepolcrale.
I casolari grigi, ammantellati
fumano intorno alla vetusta chiesa
come una breve scorta funeraria.
Or sotto i suoi lenzuoli verginali
dorme la terra aggricciata e sogna;
sogna la dolce primavera, quando
avrà l'ebbrezza pia che crea il fiore.
Bruna fata discende ora la sera,
e la campana fa la sua preghiera.*

*Il buon curato sale l'erto monte,
a un casolare povero, sepolto,
ove una madre, disseccato il pianto,
stringe al vedovo seno moribondo
un figlioletto. È freddo il focolare.
Piange l'Addolorata a capo al letto
ascoltando il vagito e il singulto.
Risponde fioca, querula, lontana
or sì, or no, morendo la campana.*

*Il buon curato sale l'erto monte,
nervoso, discosceso, solitario,
tormentato dai turbini e dal gelo.
Egli ha vinto la belva che bramisce
in noi cieca, codarda, trucolenta;
un angiol s'affaccia pe' suoi occhi,
La sua mano non sa che benedire:
le sue labbra non sanno che pregare;
ha un arcano tesoro entro il suo cuore,
che può render soave anche il dolore.*

*Il buon curato sale l'erto monte,
e tremano per lui dal ciel le stelle,
pie guardando fra le aperte nubi.
Oh quante volte per le sibilanti
balze nevose ei cade affranto! Il sangue
l'orme fiorisce di vermigli fiori.*

ANTONIO CARDINAL BACCI

La flagella la ridda aquilonare
col suo nevischio eterno lancinante;
ancor ei sale, sale dolorante....

E il buon curato è giunto all'erto monte.
Al casolare povero, sepolto
ora è cessato il pianto ed il vagito.
Risplende, come un occhio che sorride,
la finestróla. Cessa la tormenta.
Su quel candore immenso, desolato
prega, tremando, il cielo alto stellato.

THE HERO

The snow deposits its white mysteries haphazardly,
weaving riddles on every branch
in ash-like, sepulchral silence.
The gray-cloaked cottages
stand smoking around the old church
like a little funeral procession.
Under her virginal sheets
the wrinkled earth now sleeps and dreams;
it dreams of sweet spring,
when it will experience a pious flower-creating
   intoxication.
Like a dark fairy the evening now descends,
and the bell's tolling prayer to heaven above ascends.

The holy curate climbs up the mountain steep,
to a humble cottage, buried in the snow,
where a mother, with parched cry,
clutches to her widow's dying breast
a little son. The hearth is cold.
The Sorrowful Mother cries at the head of the bed
as she listens to the wail and to the sob.
The church bell's toll responds from far away,
A waning "yes" or "no" as if to say.

The holy curate climbs up the mountain steep,
nervous, dejected, solitary,
tormented by wind and frost.
He has overcome the beast that roars

within us, blind, cowardly, gory;
we see an angel looking at us through his eyes.
His hand only knows how to bless:
his lips know nothing but prayer;
within his heart a secret treasure lies,
by which, made sweet, all pain forever dies.

The holy curate climbs up the mountain steep,
and the stars tremble for him from heaven
as they piously look on through the open clouds.
Oh how many times on the whistling
snowy cliffs he falls exhausted! The blood-drops
stain his footprints with vermilion blooms.
The whirling north wind stings him
with its constant piercing sleet;
still he climbs, climbs in pain with frozen feet....

The holy curate's reached the mountain's top.
In the poor cottage, buried in snow
the crying has now stopped; there's no more woe.
Like a radiant eye the little window's bright.
The storm is over, soon descends the night.
On that immense, white mountain desolate
He, trembling, prays at starry heaven's gate.

ANTONIO CARDINAL BACCI

LA FARFALLA AZZURRA

—O farfalla d'azzurro, dimmi in quale
luogo prendesti quel tuo bel colore
onde tu porti così pinte l'ale?—
—Porta l'impronta il mio volante frale
dei fiori ond'io mi nutro.
Son la molle pervinca e il fragil lino
che m'offrono le coppe di zaffiro,
e poi quel fiorellino,
che chiamate—non ti scordar di me—
e che si specchia all'onda
d'uno stagno o d'un limpido acquitrino.
Come questa farfalla
l'anima nostra brilla e si colora,
se viva è la sorgente che l'irrora.

THE BLUE BUTTERFLY

—O blue butterfly, please, tell me where!
How came you that blue tint of yours to bear?
From whence got you those wings so fair?—
—"My fragile steering wheels bear the hue
of all the flowers I eat that are blue.
Soft Periwinkle and Linseed frail
offer me their sapphire cups without fail.
Next, after them, that little bloom,
what do you call it?—Forget Me Not, I assume—
that is reflected in the undulation
of a pond or limpid marsh of God's creation."
Like this butterfly
our soul deep color takes and truly shines,
if on a living source of food it dines.

LA BATTITURA DEI CASTAGNI. GIOIA AUTUNNALE

Son qui sul muschio soffice,
beato; lungi perdesi con dolci
richiami il canto delle coltrici
fra il frettoloso sbatter delle pertiche.
Qui intorno un popolo d'insetti corre,
fra tenui borborigmi,
e via s'affretta all'ultime bisogne,
che già cala l'inverno.
Ora l'autunno spande ovunque un lento
desio di pace. Ancor tepido è il sole,
ma qualche foglia, barellando, a terra
cade: nel ciel sono estasi di luce,
son palpiti d'amore;
ma par l'estasi pia che splende in volto
al vecchio stanco nella prece assorto:
ancor la terra ha un riso blando e mite
al dolce canto delle coglitrici,
ma sembra il riso d'una madre inferma.
Son qui, sul muschio soffice, beato.
Qui presso lieta croccola una fonte,
e sembra il lieto rider d'una sposa;
mentre sovra di me lento un castagno
paternamente stende le sue rame.
Oh belle, fra gli aperti ispidi labbri
Dei ricci biondi, le castagne baie!
Quante bocche ridenti
sgranansi fra il fogliame giallo, mentre
cade qua e là, nel riso, il dolce frutto.
O pio castagno, io mi credeva un giorno
che si nascesse nel tuo tronco bugio
come le brune Driadi;
e quando bimbo ignaro qui venivo
dentro cercavo al cortice del cavo
tronco, cogli occhi, un angioletto biondo;
pia favola per cui sempre ti ho amato
si come un vecchio nonno.
Nonno castagno, e tu serbi nell'ultima
stagione ai tuoi nepoti

negli aspri scrigni de' tuoi ricci impervi,
come nel chiuso pugno, il dolce frutto;
il dolce frutto, per cui poi gioisce
la famigliola intorno al focolare:
fuori stride l'inverno,
turbina un urlo rauco di minaccia
giù per le nere spire del camino;
ma sul ciocco borbotta la caldaia
con le brune castagne;
la nonna fila e conta le sue fole...
Il bimbo ascolta pensieroso e guarda,
con gli occhi intenti, il ciocco e la caldaia.

THE SHAKING OF THE CHESTNUT TREES.
AN AUTUMN DELIGHT

I am here on the soft moss, happy;
far off the song of the feather-poke
dies out with sweet calls
amidst the hurried smacking of the poles.
Round about a nation of insects runs,
among soft borborygmus,
and hurries to make the last preparations,
for winter is soon to descend upon us.
Now autumn spreads a lazy
desire for rest everywhere. Still the sun is warm;
only a few leaves, staggering, fall to the ground:
in the sky are ecstasies of light,
throbs of love;
but it is like the pious ecstasy that shines on the face
of a tired old man absorbed in prayer:
the earth still mildly and softly smiles
at the sweet song of the gatherers,
but it seems like a sick mother's smile.
I am here, on the soft moss, happy.
Here nearby happily bubbling is a spring,
With the happiness of a smiling bride;
while over me a chestnut tree
paternally spreads his branches.
Oh how beautiful are the bay-colored chestnuts,
visible between the open bristly lips

of the blond husks!
How many smiling mouths
open wide amidst the yellow foliage and in goes
the sweet fruit here and there into the smile.
O holy chestnut tree, once upon a time,
I used to imagine that like the brunette dryads
I had been born within your trunk that I imagined to
   be hollow,
and, still a silly child, used to come here
looking for a blond angel
inside the bark of that trunk;
a pious tale for which I have always loved you,
yes, just like an old grandfather.
Oh Grandfather Chestnut, you save the sweet fruit
enclosed within the tough caskets of your impervious
   husks
as in a closed fist, till the end of the season
for your grandchildren;
the sweet fruit,
which the little family enjoys around the hearth:
while outside the winter rages,
and a hoarse cry of menace swirls
down the black sides of the chimney;
yet on the burning log of wood
the kettle with brown chestnuts boils;
the grandmother spins and tells her stories...
the child listens thoughtfully and looks,
with intent eyes, on the log and the kettle.

ANTONIO CARDINAL BACCI

ALLA VERGINE DI LOURDES

*Vergine bianca che t'affisi al cielo
in estasi di pace,
e c'inviti a seguirti, col sorriso,
alla Patria verace:*

*Vergine, che ci chiami a un ideale,
che non e di quaggiù,
e c'infondi nel cuor quasi un bisogno
d'amare la virtù:*

*Vergine, a cui fioriscono le rose
senza le acute spine
sotto l'eburneo piede immacolato
e le grazie divine:*

*Fioriscon dalle labbra estasiate,
mentre nel dolce viso
fise le turbe, giubilando estatiche,
vedono il paradiso:*

*Deh perché non è un' oasi di cielo
così tutta la terra,
perché non sorgi, o Iride divina,
sull'ampia cieca guerra?*

*Oh allor soltanto il gelido deserto,
che la colpa e il dolore
tormentano in eterno, oh allor sarebbe
il regno dell'amore!*

TO OUR LADY OF LOURDES

O virgin pure who gav'st thyself
in peaceful ecstasy,
invite thou us to follow thee,
our home above to see.

O Virgin, Mediatrix
of things not here below,
of every loving virtue thou
in hearts a need dost sow.

White roses without thorns do bloom,
God's ivory colored sign
under thy feet, o virgin queen
of every grace divine.

Assembled crowds in ecstasy
see in thy most sweet face,
O Mother of God who reigns above,
divine and holy grace.

Why, why no quiet oasis
upon our earth entire?
O lily, rise and end for us
this blind world war so dire!

Oh then a frigid desert hell,
of sin and pain will be,
but, oh, a heaven of love as well
for everyone to see!

Con il latino a servizio di Quattro Papi
EDITR. STUDIUM, ROME, 1964[2]

ANTONIO BACCI, IN THIS BOOK DEDICATED TO A. Galli and N. Sebastiani, both of whom knew how to encourage him and guide him to the love of Latin, recalls the frequent and important direct contacts that he had with four pontiffs, Pius XI, Pius XII, John XXIII, and Paul VI. In this little work he records his defense of the Latin language and culture, with which he was much preoccupied because they were already well on the way in a process of decay. With an easy and simple style, he writes that it was on September 30, 1922 when, at Lecceto near Malmantine, the Cardinal Archbishop of Florence, the Piarist Alfonso Maria Mistrangelo, a native of Savona, summoned him to let him know that the people in Rome had asked him for a Latin scholar, "and so I thought to send

---

2 See the English translation by Anthony Lo Bello: *With Latin in the Service of the Popes* (Arouca Press, 2020).

you. You will therefore go into the Secretariat of State as a composer of Latin correspondence." Now Cardinal Mistrangelo was, in Bacci's words, "a humanist of tenacious memory and of the most immense culture". And thus in November of that same year there began the life in Rome of Bacci, a native of Giugnola, formerly teacher and superior at the seminary of Firenzuola as well as at the major seminary in Florence.

At the Vatican he was in the "service" of Pius XI from 1922 to 1939, beginning as a *minutante* at the Secretariat of State. Then, in 1931, he was nominated to be Secretary of Briefs to Princes with the responsibility of composing in Latin the letters that were to be sent to heads of state, as well as the encyclicals, the apostolic letters, the Motu Proprios, the apostolic constitutions, and the consistorial allocutions. In his book Bacci recalls the traits of Pius XI, the vast culture, the strength of character, the sharpness of mind, the remarkable intuition, and, most of all, the production of many encyclicals in the writing of which, he says, "I had the good luck to collaborate."

When Pius XI died, it was Antonio Bacci who, by reason of his office, had to write the *Oratio de eligendo Pontifice*, read before the Sacred College at the start of the Conclave for the election of the new Pope. With this eloquent address in Latin, he intended to underline both the grave situation in the world at that moment and the responsibility that was about to weigh on the cardinal electors: "The man who will be chosen will have to guide the bark of St. Peter in seas encumbered with icebergs broken off from the frightful ice pack of barbarism." While the loudspeakers were announcing the election of Pius XII to the pontifical throne, Antonio Bacci was in St. Peter's Square in the midst of a cheering crowd; his emotion was truly great, and "tears fell from my eyes." His collaboration with Pius XII was also long and marked by great reciprocal esteem and consideration. In his little volume, the official Latinist of the Church recalls and gives evidence of the great prudence of Pope Pacelli, whom he describes as "an inimitable example of polish, courtesy, and industry." Pius XII worked hard and made others work hard; he was endowed with a memory of iron similar to that of Pico della Mirandola In this regard, Antonio Bacci tells the following story:

> I had composed in haste (which was against his explicit instructions) an extremely long Latin discourse which the Holy Father was to pronounce shortly before a large audience in the Courtyard of San Damaso. I myself was at this audience. He began to recite this long discourse without the manuscript in his hands, as if he were improvising as he was going along. I was astounded, and when, a few days afterwards, I had the occasion to be summoned to an audience to draft some papers, I could not refrain from expressing my wonder at what had happened. But he, smiling, said, "You know, by the grace of God, when I read a discourse three times, even if it is in Latin, I can easily recite it from memory. What is more, perhaps it escaped your notice that while I was reciting that speech, I skipped over a section that appeared too long to me, given that very few can understand classical Latin when they hear it, unless they know what to expect." I replied that I had indeed noticed it, but that the speech went well enough even with that omission.

Pope Pacelli always kept at his disposal on his desk a copy of the Latin-German Dictionary of Karl Ernst Georges (1806–1895), which he consulted with a certain frequency; it was he who encouraged the Latinist from Giugnola, given the times and with them the necessity of the introduction into the Italian language of numerous neologisms, to carry through to its conclusion the composition of his *Vocabolario italiano-latino delle parole moderne*.

On the occasion of the death of Pius XII, for whom he had translated encyclicals, apostolic letters and constitutions, consistorial and extra-consistorial allocutions, and radio messages, it fell to the Secretary of Briefs to compose, in his beautiful Latin, the funeral elegy and the four Latin inscriptions located at the four sides of the catafalque.

Once again, after the death of Pope Pacelli, Antonio Bacci received the assignment to compose and read before the assembled cardinals the *Oratio de eligendo Pontifice*. His was not a formal discourse but instead presented a pressing invitation to the electors to keep in mind the particularly difficult moment in which the Church had need of a true pastor, a man ready to receive the bishops and to put into practice the documents and social encyclicals of the Popes; he would have to be a bridge between all nations, even those that persecuted Catholics. "A learned Pope is not enough," he concluded his exhortation; "a Pope who knows the human and divine sciences and who has explored the subtle ways of diplomacy and politics will not suffice. All these things are necessary, but they are not sufficient. What is needed is a Pope who is a saint, because a Pope who is a saint can obtain from God even that which natural gifts do not grant." "Many cardinals," wrote the Vatican expert Benny Lai on January 21, 1971, "entered the conclave with their copies of Bacci's speech here and there underlined, and they came out having given the white habit to Angelo Roncalli."

After the election of the *good Pope* in the evening scrutiny, Bacci had a long late-night meeting with him to prepare the radio message in Latin that the newly elected Pope had to give on the following day.

> I found the new Pope serene and tranquil, just as I had seen him years before at Castel Gandolfo in the Pontifical Antechamber before my audience. It was that full and complete serenity that only absolute faith and total abandonment to the will of God can give.

So writes Cardinal Bacci in his book, which records his concrete and busy collaboration with the new Pope, marked by many extended, spontaneous, and fraternal conversations. Most important were the documents of John XXIII such as the encyclicals *Ad Petri Cathedram*, *Mater et Magistra*, and *Pacem in Terris*; they had a great resonance, and not only in the Catholic world. The name of Pope Roncalli is linked most of all with the summoning of the Second Vatican Ecumenical Council. About this Cardinal Bacci writes:

> It was an act of great courage, the courage of one who sees everything from the point of view of Deity and who determines to move ahead in spite of obstacles and difficulties.... It was like (and so it appeared to all) a great window opened up to let the sun shine on the world,... *Ut omnes unum sint... Et fiet unum ovile et unus pastor,...*

However—it was June 3, 1963—the good Pope was now no more.

The successor chosen by the cardinal electors was Giovanni Battista Montini, Archbishop of Milan, who assumed the name of Paul VI. The weighty inheritance of the Council—writes Bacci—was handled by Paul VI with intelligence, heart, and will. The relations between the new Pontiff and the *Latin Cardinal* were marked by reciprocal and profound esteem.

The latter writes:

> Since I became a cardinal in the last years of John XXIII and was therefore no longer Latin Secretary of Briefs to Princes, my service to the Popes has taken on a different nature. Even though, once in a while, I am still invited, in exceptional cases, to help out in drawing up Pontifical documents, my major contribution now takes place in the four Sacred Congregations of which I am a member, the Sacred Congregation of the Council, the Sacred Congregation of Religious, the Sacred Congregation of Rites, and the Sacred Congregation of Seminaries and Universities. What is more, I have made my contribution as a Council Father in the deliberations of Vatican II, as best as my limitations allow, by exhorting in particular that we avoid all imprecision and ambiguity of language, which, in such solemn and important acts, might generate confusion, damage, and danger.

This little volume, precious and fluid, contains other brief chapters in which Antonio Bacci treats of the use of Latin and the kind of Latin to be used in the conciliar documents. Some pages are also dedicated to the sort of Latin that ought to be taught in the schools.

Lexicon eorum vocabulorum quae difficilius latine redduntur.
SOCIETAS LIBRARIA "STUDIUM", ROME 1955.

AMONG THE PUBLICATIONS OF BACCI, *LEXICON eorum vocabulorum quae difficilius latine redduntur* (*Vocabolario italiano-latino delle parole modern e difficili a tradurre*), published in 1944 in Rome by the Societas Libraria "Studium", is a work truly unique as an interesting and necessary completion of the *Lessico* of Egidio Forcellini (1688-1768). In this work of his, the Latinist from Giugnola, who was in the service of four Popes (Pius XI, Pius XII, John XXIII, and Paul VI) for whom he composed in Latin the encyclicals and "briefs", that is, the papal documents at one time sent to the princes of reigning houses, efficaciously rendered difficult-to-translate modern words in the language of Cicero. One must note that even some words from English that have become the common patrimony of Italians are there brilliantly and sympathetically rendered into Latin. That the Dictionary is a specialized and especially needed work the Cardinal himself affirms when in the preface he writes:

> The *Lexicon*... is not intended to be a work perfect and complete in its genre, although I have taken great pains and devoted great passion and much labor to it... we are dealing with a small matter, but, while Latin is almost everywhere at the point of being extinguished, it seems to me — at least if I am not mistaken — that my efforts will probably be of some use.

This was the wish of Bacci, who was the *cultor et amator* of "his" Latin even to the point of later writing, "though with some reservations", the preface to the little book *La tunica stracciata. Lettere di un cattolico sulla "Riforma liturgica"* of Tito Casini, his fellow Tuscan of almost the same age, in which the author, originally from Cornacchiaia, took a drastic position against the reform desired by the Second Vatican Ecumenical Council, maintaining that the liturgy was "levelled to the ground" and that with regard to Latin they were wreaking havoc. The *Vocabolario* very much pleased the cultured Giovanni Battista Montini who — it was November 9, 1944 — sent the Cardinal a letter from the Secretariat of State in which the future Paul VI declared himself *summopere gratulatus* both for the gift itself as for its uniqueness; he furthermore expressed the wish that the literary labors of Monsignor Bacci would provide the stimulus and incentive, especially to the men of the Roman Curia, to study the Latin language in depth so as to know it and enjoy it. Perhaps, if it were the same Antonio Bacci, the authentic *praeclarus Latinitatis cultor*, who had to compose the Latin with which the Osservatore Romano announced to the world, in a special edition, the election to the pontificate of Karol Woityla, there would not have been written the words *sibi nominem (sic) imposuit*.... to indicate that the new Pope had adopted the name *John Paul II*. And here the concoction *nominem* was not correct; in fact, in Latin the noun *nomen, nominis* is neuter, and words of that gender have the same ending in the nominative, vocative, and accusative cases. *Ergo*—just to continue with the Latin—the correct form was and is *nomen*. And by the way, in the matter of blunders, and (as one often says nowadays), *par conditio*—to give equal treatment—infelicities of this sort have not only affected the Vatican; even the experts of the *Romana Studiorum Universitas "Sapientia"* were no less wrong when they announced the conferral of an honorary degree *in utroque iure* to John Paul II. On the parchment, in fact, instead of the words *Nos Iosephus D'Ascenzo rector iuris facultatis...*, which would have been correct, there appeared the words *iuris facultatem (sic)*, this last word being declined as an incomprehensible accusative instead of the genitive. The late Polish Pope was a victim for the second time. Here is a significant oddity: Ettore Maffacini, in a remark about his wonderful *Pinoculus... in latinum sermonem conversus*, writes, "I cannot refrain from mentioning the names of the illustrious humanists Msgr. Alberto Costa, Bishop of Lecce, and Msgr. Antonio Bacci, Secretary of Briefs to Princes, who sympathetically read and approved of this work." Thus, one can say that even for experts, the Cardinal from Giugnola represented a secure point of reference.

In what follows, we present some neologisms coined by the "Latin Cardinal", excerpted right from his *Lexicon eorum vocabulorum quae difficilius latine redduntur*, that is, from his *Vocabolario italiano-latino delle parole moderne e difficili a tradurre*:

ANTONIO CARDINAL BACCI

AGRICULTURAL COOPERATIVE	=	*Adiutrix societas in agris colendis*
AIRPLANE	=	*Velivolum, Aeronavis*
ANTICLERICAL	=	*Clericorum osor*
ANTIPASTO	=	*Gustatio*
ARMOURED CAR	=	*Automatarius currus loricatus*
ARMORED CRUISERS	=	*Loricata navis speculatoria*
AUTOMOBILE	=	*Autocinetum*
AVALANCHE	=	*Ingens nivium glomus e monte delapsum*
BACON OMELETTE	=	*Placenta ovorum intrita cum frustis carnium*
BANK	=	*Mensa argentaria*
BAR	=	*Taberna potoria*
BATHROOM	=	*Latrina defluente aqua instructa*
BICYCLE	=	*Birota*
BIDET	=	*Mannulus*
BLACK MARKET	=	*Annona excandefacta*
BOILED MEAT	=	*Caro elixa*
BOMB (verb)	=	*Ignivomis globis verberare*
BORROW MONEY	=	*Sumere pecunias mutuas*
BOY SCOUT	=	*Puer explorator*
BRAKES	=	*Sufflamina*
BRIBE	=	*Aere domare*
BRIGADIER	=	*Praefectus manipularis*
BRITISH COMMONWEALTH	=	*Britannicae communitatis dominia*
BUSTLE	=	*Occursatio et discursatio hominum*
CABINET (government)	=	*Supremum Consilium publicae rei administrandae*
CASHIER	=	*Nummularius*
CENTRIFUGAL	=	*Mediam partem fugiens*
CENTRIPETAL	=	*Mediam partem petens*
CHAUVINISM	=	*Immodicus suae patriae amor*
CHOCOLATE	=	*Teobroma*
CLASS STRUGGLE	=	*Civium ordinum inter ipsos dimicatio*
COCAINE	=	*Cocae pulvis*
COFFEE	=	*Potio arabica*
COLANDER	=	*Pastae colum*
COLD (CHILL)	=	*Narium destillatio*

The Works of Antonio Cardinal Bacci

COMMUNIST	=	*Aequationis bonorum fautor*
CONDOLENCE	=	*Commiseratio*
COSMOPOLITE (world citizen)	=	*Mundi civis et incola*
COTECHINO (a highly spiced sausage)	=	*Lucanica*
TO COUNTERFEIT MONEY	=	*Nummos adulterare*
CRIMINAL RECORD	=	*Probitatis documentum*
CROUTON	=	*Crustulum*
CYCLIST	=	*Birotularius*
DEMAGOGUE	=	*Seditiosus plebis ductor*
DERAIL	=	*Ex ferratae viae ductibus exire*
DIAERESIS	=	*Syllabae divisio*
DRIVER	=	*Autoraedarius*
ELECTRIC SHAVER	=	*Novacula electride acta*
EMBROIDERED LACE	=	*Pinnatum*
EQUATOR	=	*Circulus aequinoctialis*
EROTOMANIA	=	*Libidinis furor*
EUPHEMISM	=	*Locutionis mitigatio*
EXCOMMUNICATION	=	*Sacrorum communionis privatio*
EYE GLASSES	=	*Vitra ocularia*
FEMINISM	=	*Aequandus mulierum hominumque status*
FEUD	=	*Jus ultionis*
FLATULENCE	=	*Stomachi vel intestini inflatio*
FLOUR	=	*Puls*
FOREIGN MINISTRY	=	*Supremum Consilium exteris rei publicae negotiis praepositum*
FREELOADER	=	*Homo tardus et inutilis*
GAS MASK	=	*Persona contra letiferos flatus praemuniens*
GIVE AN ULTIMATUM	=	*Extremas condiciones imponere*
GNOCCHI WITH TOMATO SAUCE	=	*Convoluti pastilli lycopersico suco conditi*
GOLD INGOT	=	*Auri lingula*
GRINDER	=	*Pistrilla*

ANTONIO CARDINAL BACCI

HELIOTHERAPY = *Solaris curatio*
HIDE IN AMBUSH IN THE WOODS = *In silvis latere*
HIPPODROME = *Equorum stadium*
HYDROPHOBIA = *Aquae pavor*
HYPODERMAL INJECTION = *Injectio intercus*

ICEBERG = *Natans glaciata moles*
ICONOGRAPHY = *Imaginum descriptio*
IDENTITY CARD = *Chartula imaginem alicuius referens*
IMPERIALISM = *Imperii amplificandi studium*
INKWELL = *Atramentarium*
INVEST MONEY = *Pecuniam in praedio collocare*
IRON GIRDER = *Ferrea trabs*

JUDICIAL ENQUIRY = *Cognitio causae*

LAND REGISTRY = *Publica census tabula*
LEADER = *Ductor*
LIFT (elevator) = *Pegma scansorium*
LITHOGRAPH (TO MAKE A—) = *In lapide incisum imprimere*
LOTTERY TICKETS = *Scidulae aleatoriae*

MACARONI = *Pasta tabulata*
MACHINE GUN = *Manuballistarius*
MARZOCCO (heraldic lion) = *Florentini leonis insignia*
MATCH (to light a cigarette) = *Sulphuratum*
MENTAL HOSPITAL = *Dementium valetudinarium*
MERCHANT SHIP = *Navis mercatoria*
METAMORPHOSIS = *Formae mutatio*
MILITARISM = *Nimium bellandi studium*
MINE FIELD = *Ager ignivomis consitus globis*
MINISTRY OF EDUCATION = *Supremum Consilium publicae institutioni praepositum*
MINISTRY OF FINANCE = *Supremum Consilium rebus vectigalibus praepositum*
MINISTRY OF PUBLIC WORKS = *Supremum Consilium publicis operibus praepositum*
MISCELLANY = *Miscellania*
MONETARY INFLATION = *Charta nummaria nimia ac vilescens*
MORTADELLA = *Myrtatum farcimen*

The Works of Antonio Cardinal Bacci

MUEZZIN = *Sacer Arabum praeco*
MUSICAL OPERETTA = *Fabula ludicra musica ornata*
MYTHOLOGY = *Historia fabularis*
NAZI = *Exagitatus ac praepotens nationis suae fautor*
NECROMANCY = *Mortuorum evocatio*
NEPHRITIS = *Inflammatio renum*
NERVOUS BREAKDOWN = *Debilitatio nervorum*
NEUTRALITY = *Studium nullius partis*
NUMISMATICS = *Veteres recentioresque nummi in ordinem redacti*

OBITUARY = *Funebre nuntium*
OVEREAT = *Se ingurgitare*

PAWNSHOP = *Mensa pigneratitia*
PAY OFF A LOAN = *Aes mutuum reddere*
PEDOMETER = *Mensorius itineris index*
PHARMACY = *Medicamentaria taberna*
POSTAGE STAMP = *Pittacium cursuale*
PROMISE THE MOON = *Maria montesque polliceri*
PROMISSORY NOTE = *Syngrapha*
PROOFS = *Paginae emendandae*

RADIO NEWSPAPER = *Radiophonicum diurnorum actorum nuntium*
RAVEGGIOLO (a soft white cheese) = *Caseus molliculus*
RESIGNATION OF THE GOVERNMENT = *Rei publicae rectionis abdicatio*
ROAST VEAL = *Assum vitulinum*
ROTISSERIE = *Machinatio carnibus assandis*

SALAD DRESSED WITH OLIVE OIL AND VINEGAR = *Acetaria*
SANDWICH = *Pastillum farctum*
SAUSAGE = *Botulus*
SEASONAL RICE PADDY WORKER = *Oryzae purgatrix*
SELL AT A DISCOUNT = *Ex pecunia deductionem facere*
SEWING MACHINE = *Machina consuens*

ANTONIO CARDINAL BACCI

SHOWER = *Balneae pensiles*
SKYSCRAPERS = *Caelum perfricantes aedes*
SOCCER = *Follis pedumque ludus*
SOVIET UNION = *Foederatae communistarum Russiae Respublicae*
SPAGHETTI = *Pasta vermiculata*
SPEEDBOAT = *Navigium automatarium*
STEAMING HOT CUP OF COFFEE = *Fumantis cafaei pocillum*
STEERING WHEEL = *Moderatrix raedae automataria rotula*
STONES (DISEASE) = *Calculorum morbus*
SWEETMEAT (TOFFEE) = *Mellitus pastillus*

TELEVISION = *Televisificum instrumentum*
THROMBOSIS = *Arteriae vel venae sanguinis coagulatio*
TOMATO CONSERVE (preserves) = *Lycopersici decoctum*
TORTELLI WITH SAUCE AND CHEESE = *Pilei esculenti suco pulveratoque caseo conditi*
TOURISM = *Peregrinationes delectationis causa susceptae*
TOWN COUNCIL = *Consilium curatorum rei municipalis*
TYPEWRITER = *Dactylographicum prelum*

UNCONSTITUTIONAL = *Primariae rei publicae legi discors*
UNEMPLOYMENT = *Coacta operis vacatio*
UNIVERSITY STUDENTS = *Juvenes athenaea frequentantes*
USURER = *Fenerator*

VERMOUTH = *Vinum absinthio conditum*

WATER WORKS = *Machinae aquas vorantes*
WIN THE LOTTERY = *Prospera sortium alea uti*
WRITE WITH A PENCIL = *Scriptorio lapide exarare*

XENOPHOBIA = *Odium in externos*
XYLOGRAPHY = *Imago ex lignea scalptura*

YACHT = *Pamphilum navigium*

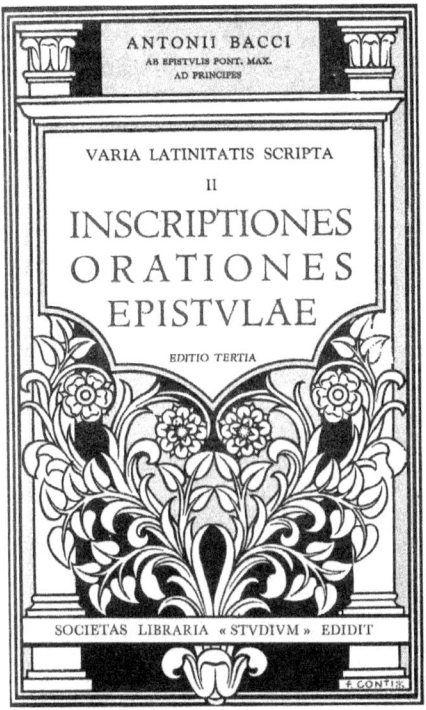

Inscriptiones Orationes Epistulae.
SOCIETAS LIBRARIA "STUDIUM", ROME 1944

IN THIS INTERESTING PUBLICATION THAT appeared in the same year as the *Vocabolario*, the Cardinal demonstrates a deep knowledge and a singular command of the Latin language in combination with a special poetic streak. His brief texts, especially those referring to members of his family, to the environment and aspects of his native region, and to his friends are evidence of vast erudition. They are also an obvious confirmation of that fruitful capacity for composing, by means of sentiment and poetry, sketches of family, town, and even curial life. His brief compositions are pleasing and capable and arouse the admiration of the reader;

he writes them in that Latin of his that is clean, simple, and refined all at once.

The book, copies of which he sent to Pius XII and Giovanni Battista Montini at the Secretariat of State, were particularly appreciated by the latter, who sent a letter, written in Latin, whose partial contents, freely translated, sound like this:

> May Heaven grant that in ever greater numbers, those members of the clergy, but at the same time and especially those belonging to the Roman Curia, be stimulated and motivated, following this special example of yours, to dedicate themselves to an ever more frequent use of the Latin language, so that even in our times it may not cease to be loved, to be well cultivated, and to thrive.

In what follows we present some inscriptions, especially those relating to Giugnola, where he was born, to Piancaldoli, where he contributed to the founding of the local Savings and Loan Association, and to Firenzuola, the small town where he was a student in the archiepiscopal seminary. A translation appears below each Latin text.

The Works of Antonio Cardinal Bacci

*Francisco Pifferi sacerdoti,
curiae Plancalidi Praeposito*

QVOD · PIVS · XII · PONT · MAX
INTER · CVBICVLARIOS · SVOS · INTIMOS
HONORIS · CAVSSA
TE · MERENTEM · COOPTAVIT
MECVM · OMNES · QVOTQVOT · HABES · AESTIMATORES
GRATVLANTVR
CVM · EX · MONTANA · PLANCALIDI · CVRIA
FRANCISCI · PIFFERI · SAC
ROMAM · VSQVE · PERVENISSE · CERNANT
VIRTVTIS · NOMEN
A · MDCCCCXXXXV

* * *

*To the Priest Francesco Pifferi,
Provost of the Parish of Piancalidi*

BECAUSE PIUS XII SUPREME PONTIFF
APPOINTED YOU AN HONORARY PRIVY CHAMBERLAIN
ALL YOUR ADMIRERS JOIN ME
IN CONGRATULATING YOU.
THE REPUTATION OF THE PRIEST FRANCESCO PIFFERI
MADE IT
FROM THE MOUNTAINS OF THE PARISH OF PIANCALDOLI.
ALL THE WAY TO ROME.
IN THE YEAR 1945.

ANTONIO CARDINAL BACCI

*Supra rusticum fontem
in Etruriae Aemiliaeque finibus*

IGNOTVS · QVONDAM · LATEX
EX · OCCVLTIS · TERRAE · VISCERIBVS
HAC · SVB · ALTA · QVERCV
TANDEM · PVRA · LYMPHA · SCATEO
VBI
FRITINNIENTES · AVES · CERNO · PECVDESQVE · BALANTES
SVAM · SORBILLANDO · RESTINGVERE · SITIM
TV · ITEM · REQVIESCE
PARVMPER · HEIC · VIATOR · AC · BIBE
DVMQVE · DVLCISSIMI · CIRCVMQVAQVE · VOLVCRES
CANTIBVS · AETHERA · MVLCENT
SERENA · TE · PACE · BEANS
CLAMOSAS · OBLIVISCERE · VRBES
TVRBVLENTAMQVE · VITAM
AN · A · REP · SAL · MDCCCCXXXXVI

* * *

*Above a rustic spring at
the border of Tuscany and Emilia*

ONCE A LIQUID OF UNKNOWN ORIGIN
PROCEEDING FROM THE INNERMOST BOWELS OF THE EARTH
UNDER THIS TALL OAK TREE
I NOW FINALLY GUSH FORTH
PURE SPRING WATER
AND WATCH THE SIPPING AND CHIRPING
BIRDS AND FROLICKING CATTLE
QUENCH THEIR THIRST.
YOU TOO NOW RELAX HERE FOR A WHILE
DEAR TRAVELLER
AND DRINK
AS ALL AROUND THE DELIGHTFUL WINGED TRIBE
SOOTHES THE AIR WITH THEIR SONGS.
BE GLAD FOR THIS SERENE PEACE
AND FORGET THE NOISY CITIES AND YOUR TROUBLED LIFE.
IN THE YEAR 1946 AFTER THE
ACCOMPLISHMENT OF OUR SALVATION

The Works of Antonio Cardinal Bacci
Plancalidi, in oppidulo prope
Etruriae Aemiliaeque fines

SACRAM · HANC · AEDEM
INCREBRESCENTI · POPVLO · ANGVSTAM
TEMPORVMQVE · INIVRIA · FATISCENTEM
AVSPICE · EM · VIRO · A · M · MISTRANGELO · CARD
FLORENTINORVM · PONTIFICE
ARCHITECTO · E · BELLETTI · CAESENATE
FRANCISCVS · PIFFERI · CVRIAE · PRAEPOSITVS
SVIS · POPVLIQVE · SVMPTIBVS
MOLE · AMPLIORE
REFICIENDAM
MVSIVIS · CAELATISQVE · OPERIBVS · EXORNANDAM
CVRAVIT
ANNO · A · REP · SAL · MDCCCCXXV

* * *

At Piancalidi, a little town on
the border of Tuscany and Emilia

THIS SACRED TEMPLE
TOO SMALL FOR THE EVER INCREASING MULTITUDE
DILAPIDATED FROM THE RAVAGES OF TIME
UNDER THE PATRONAGE OF A. M. CARDINAL MISTRANGELO
ARCHBISHOP OF FLORENCE
AND UNDER THE SUPERVISION OF THE
ARCHITECT E. BELLETTI OF CESENA
FRANCESCO PIFFERI THE PARISH PRIEST
AT HIS OWN EXPENSE AND WITH THE
CONTRIBUTIONS OF THE PEOPLE
RENOVATED AND ENLARGED
AND BEAUTIFIED WITH MOSAICS AND ENGRAVINGS
IN THE YEAR 1925 AFTER THE ACCOMPLISHMENT
OF OUR SALVATION [3]

---

[3] "Three altars of Bergamo marble adorn the church, and the main altar erected at the expense of the Rural Savings and Loan Association is beautiful in its simplicity." (*Piancaldoli, Memorie storico-artistiche*, S. Gaddoni and A. Marrani, G. Pagnini Edit., Florence, 1990.)

ANTONIO CARDINAL BACCI

Juniolae, in Bononiensis Provinciae oppidulo

SACELLVM · HOC
TRIBVS · LAPIDEIS · ARIS · SVFFECTIS
AFFABREQVE · INSCVLPTIS
CONTIGNATIONE · OPPORTVNE · REPARATA
AC · FENESTRIS · APTIVS · RESTITVTIS
FRANCISCVS · GALEOTTI · CVRIO
SVIS · POPVLIQVE · IMPENSIS
INSTAVRAVIT
ANNO · A · REP · SAL · MDCCCCXXIV

* * *

At Giugnola, a small town in the province of Bologna

THIS SANCTUARY
PROVIDED WITH THREE STONE ALTARS SKILLFULLY ENGRAVED
WITH THE FLOOR SUITABLY REPAIRED
AND THE WINDOWS PROPERLY FIXED
WAS RENOVATED BY
FRANCESCO GALEOTTI THE PASTOR
AT HIS OWN EXPENSE AND THAT OF THE PEOPLE
IN THE YEAR 1924 AFTER THE
ACCOMPLISHMENT OF OUR SALVATION

* * *

In membrane, quae colorum luminibus exornata, et in ferreo tabulo inclusa, ad fundamenta sacri Florentiolae Seminarii deposita fuit, iterum excitandi

SACRVM · FLORENTIOLAE · SEMINARIVM
QVOD · ANTONIVS · MARTINI · FLOR · ARCHIEPISCOPVS
PRO · MONTANIS · ARCHIODIOECESEOS · REGIONIBVS
NON · SINE · DEI · NVTV · CONDIDERAT
QVODQVE · PER · IMMANE · BELLVM
IGNIVOMIS · E · CAELO · DEIECTIS · GLOBIS
CORRVPTVM · AC · DIRVTVM · IACVERAT
EM · VIR · ELIAS · DALLA · COSTA · S · R · E · CARD
EIVSDEMQVE · ARCHID · ANTISTES

The Works of Antonio Cardinal Bacci

BONORVM · OBSECVNDANS · VOTIS
FELICITER · INCHOAVIT
AC · LAPIDEM · AVSPICALEM
AB · SE · RITE · EXPIATVM
POSVIT
ID · A · PASTORVM · PRINCIPE · EFFLAGITANS
VT · HINC · SACERDOTES · QVAM · PLVRIMI
BENESVADAE · VIRGINIS · CONSILIO · CONFORMATI
OMNIVMQVE · VIRTVTVM · FVLGORE · PRAESTANTES
ITERVM · EXSISTERENT
A · MDCCCCLIII

* * *

On the parchment scroll which, illustrated in color and inserted into an iron canister, was deposited in the foundation of the holy seminary of Firenzuola as it was about to be rebuilt

THE HOLY SEMINARY OF FIRENZUOLA THAT
ANTONIO MARTINI
ARCHBISHOP OF FLORENCE
NOT WITHOUT THE DIVINE APPROBATION
ESTABLISHED FOR THE MOUNTAINOUS
REGIONS OF HIS ARCHDIOCESE
AND WHICH DURING A HORRIBLE WAR
WAS DAMAGED AND THEN LEVELLED
BY FIRE BOMBS THAT FELL FROM THE SKY
HIS EMINENCE ELIA DALLA COSTA
CARDINAL OF THE HOLY ROMAN CHURCH
PASTOR OF THE SAME ARCHDIOCESE
ACCEDING TO THE WISHES OF THE GOOD PEOPLE
HAPPILY TOOK THE FIRST STEP TO REBUILD
AND LAID THE CORNER STONE WHICH HE HAD BLESSED
AND ASKED THIS OF THE PRINCE OF THE APOSTLES
THAT FROM HERE AS MANY PRIESTS AS POSSIBLE
CONFORMING TO THE WILL OF OUR LADY OF GOOD COUNSEL
NOTEWORTHY FOR THE LUSTER OF ALL THEIR VIRTUES
MIGHT ONCE AGAIN GO FORTH
IN THE YEAR 1953

ANTONIO CARDINAL BACCI

Nataliae, sorori meae desideratissimae carissimaeque

SVAVISSIMAE · MEMORIAE
NATALIAE · BACCI
QVAE
ANIMI · CANDOREM · VIRGINEO · REFERENS · ADSPECTV
HILARIQVE · VVLTV
PARENTBVS · FRATRIBVS · SORORIBVS
IN · DELICIIS · ERAT
AT · LETALI · MORBO · IMPLICITA
MENTEM · EX · OCCIDVA · HAC · VITA
AD · CAELESTIA · ERIGENS
OBITV · PIISSIMO · AD · SVPEROS · EVOLAVIT
DECESSIT · A · MDCCCLXXXXVI
AETATI · SVAE · XVII
ELATAQVE POPVLARI LVCTV
DVM EX AVTVMNALIBVS ARBORIBVS
STILLANTIA FOLIA CADEBANT
EX OMNIVMQVE OCVLIS LACRIMAE

* * *

To my dearest and sorely missed sister Natalia

TO THE MOST SWEET MEMORY OF
NATALIA BACCI
WHO ADDED A SINCERE HEART
TO HER VIRGIN PRESENCE AND SMILING FACE.
SHE WAS THE DELIGHT OF HER
PARENTS, BROTHERS AND SISTERS
BUT STRUCK DOWN WITH A MORTAL ILLNESS
SHE TURNED HER MIND AWAY FROM THIS TRANSIENT EXISTENCE
TO THE ETERNAL LIFE OF PARADISE.
AFTER A PIOUS DEATH SHE ASCENDED TO THE WORLD ABOVE
SHE DIED IN THE YEAR 1896
AT SEVENTEEN YEARS OF AGE
TO WIDESPREAD POPULAR GRIEF
AND AS THE AUTUMN LEAVES FELL FROM THE TREES
TEARS FLOWED FROM OUR EYES

The Works of Antonio Cardinal Bacci

Hectori fraterculo meo dulcissimo

HECTOR · BACCI
CAELO · POTIVS · QVAM · MVNDO · NATVS
VNA · SOLVMMODO · HORA · VIVENS
ADSTANTIBVS
ARRISIT · ILLACRIMAVIT · OBIITQVE
A · MDCCCLXXXVII
SALVE · AETERNVM · IN · CHRISTO

* * *

To my sweet little brother Ettore

ETTORE BACCI
MEANT FOR THE NEXT WORLD RATHER THAN FOR THIS
HAVING LIVED JUST ONE HOUR
SMILED, BEGAN TO CRY, AND THEN DIED
IN THE YEAR 1887
HAIL FOREVER IN CHRIST

Candele che si spengono.
Dalla Parrocchia di montana
alla Curia Romana.[4]

A. BELARDETTI EDIT., ROME, 1953

IN THIS BOOK, DON ANTONIO BACCI TALKS about his life as a young priest destined for pastoral service as assistant to the pastor of Casetta di Tiara, a needy section of the commune of Palazzuolo di Romagna (today Palazzuolo sul Senio) of the Vicariate of Firenzuola. Stories are presented and characters described in a polished and pleasing Italian that has the bonus of being delightful to read. Unfortunately, in reporting the names of persons and places, the future cardinal

---

4 *Candles that go out: From a mountain parish to the Roman Curia*

has used ("for delicacy" he says) pseudonyms for both. This expedient, at a distance of so many years, can presents certain difficulties for the reader.

There emerges from his pages the edifying figure of the pastor of the time, Don Carlino Tagliaferri, so similar to the Curé d'Ars. Here is the description of him that, in the opinion of some elderly local people, was absolutely accurate:

> He looked like Saint Anthony of Padua, withered, with a face molded by toil and hardship, but with two lively scintillating eyes like those of a child. He had been up there among those steep cliffs for about fifty years devoting his whole being to the good of his people, and not only for their spiritual wellbeing, but also for their material welfare. When he learned that some poor family was in need of help to work its meager land and was unable to pay for hired hands, he set his breviary aside and grabbed the spade or hoe, he donned his rough bell-shaped cassock, he secured it around his waist with a belt, and went out with the peasants to do his share, and he knew how to do it... The parish church had no endowment, only a poor but adequate vegetable garden which he worked himself... And yet, despite these economic hardships,... eating nothing more than polenta and vegetables, often taking, as they say, a bite out of his mouth, he succeeded in building the new church, in raising that strong bell tower of gray sandstone, and in restoring the rectory.

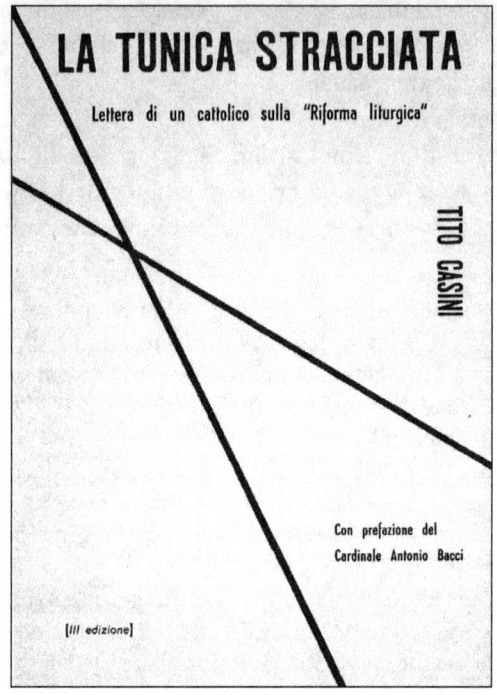

Preface of Antonio Cardinal Bacci to the book La Tunica stracciata: Lettera di un cattolico sulla "Riforma liturgica"

BY TITO CASINI, SATES, ROME, 1967[5]

I HAVE BEEN INVITED TO WRITE A BRIEF INTROduction to this little book by Tito Casini.

I cannot decline, nor do I want to decline; in fact, I write this willingly although with some reservations. I have known Tito Casini from my earliest youth and prize him as one of the best Catholic authors in Italy. His style is fresh, frank, and sincere and reminds me of the pure mountain air of my (and his) Firenzuola, and he is a staunch Christian. I can repeat

---

5 This book was republished by Angelico Press in 2020 as *The Torn Tunic: Letter of a Catholic on the "liturgical Reform."*

of him what an ancient sacred author once said of himself, "*Christianus mihi nomen, catholicus cognomen.*" Finally, I can also write this because although his book may seem a bit irreverent to some, all must recognize that it has been dictated only by a burning love for the Church and for liturgical decorum.

One can and must affirm that nothing that he writes in this little volume is ever contrary to what the Second Vatican Council declared in its Constitution on the Liturgy; rather he opposes the practical implementation that certain raving and exaggerating innovators would like to do at any cost, not to speak of what some are doing on this slippery slope with their so-called Eucharistic banquets, rock masses, polka masses, hippy masses, and "similar trash".

I write this willingly, I repeat, because I believe that these pages, which bring to mind those even more fiery, bold, and unprejudiced pages of Saint Catherine of Siena, can correct some ideas and do some good.

I trust that those interested will generously pardon the author for certain sentences which may seem rude to them and remember that these lines were composed not to offend, but only because the author's heart was exacerbated by certain novelties that seemed and indeed are outright profanations.

What is more, in this book there is something to learn for everyone, something that comes from the voice of the laity, especially from those laymen, like Tito Casini, who are perfect Catholics.

And here I can do no less than mention that an International Federation has been formed for the safeguard of Latin and Gregorian Chant in the Catholic liturgy, a Federation that numbers among its members innumerable people from eleven countries and with its headquarters in Zürich, Switzerland.

This Federation publishes a newsletter with the Latin name *Una Voce*, a phrase which for us can also be Italian, because our national language, as has been said, is nearly a dialect of Latin, and the Latin of the liturgy, heir of the *sermo rusticus* spoken long ago by the common folk, can be easily understood, at least in great part, better certainly than certain barbarous translations that are examples of the truth of that saying that a translator is a traitor.

In this year's January issue the aforementioned newsletter asserts that "it seems one's duty to denounce certain situations which do not correspond in any way with the renewal desired by the Council." The conciliar Constitution referred to above established as a general principle the preservation of Latin in the sacred rites (article 36.1), at the same time conceding the use of the vernacular language in the readings and in certain parts of the Mass to be determined, in case this would be useful for the greater understanding of the people. But the total and exclusive use of the vernacular language, as is the case in the many parts of Italy, not only goes contrary to the Council but is also the cause of spiritual suffering for a great part of the people.

I therefore think that the petition presented by the Italian branch of the International Association to the Italian Episcopal Conference for the safeguarding of the Latin language and of sacred music in the Catholic liturgy deserves to be received with attentive and favorable consideration so that it not happen that while the Mass and the other sacred rites are celebrated in bad Italian and even in Esperanto, Latin—the official language of the Church—is totally banned from the sacred rites like something leprous.

It seems, therefore, opportune that at least in cathedral churches, in sanctuaries, in tourist centers, and everywhere where there is a sufficient number of clergy, there be celebrated at least some Masses in Latin according to an established schedule in correspondence with the just wishes of those—foreigners and Italians—who prefer Latin to the vernacular language and Gregorian Chant to musical rubbish that is nowadays with little propriety ever more replacing it in Catholic worship.

Vatican City
February 23, 1967

BIBLIOGRAPHY

Bacci, Antonio, *Oasi: Rime e ritmi giovanili*, Ars Italica Edit., Naples, 1915.

—, *Candele che si spengono: Dalla parrocchia di montagna alla Curia Romana*, A. Bellardetti Edit., Rome, 1953.

—, *Vocabolario italiano-latino delle parole moderne e difficili a tradurre*, Soc. Libr. "Studium" Ed., Rome, 1955.

—, *Inscriptiones orationes epistulae*, Soc. Libr. "Studium" Ed., Rome, 1955.

—, *Con il latino a servizio di Quattro Papi*, Editrice Studium, Rome, 1964.

Casini, Stefano, *Dizionario geografico biografico storico del Comune di Firenzuola*, Tip. Campolini, Florence, 1914.

Casini, Tito, *La tunica stracciata: Lettera di un cattolico sulla "Riforma liturgica"*, SATES Edit., Rome, 1967.

Collodi, Carlo, *Pinoculus liber qui inscribitur "Le avventure di Pinocchio" auctore C. Collodi in latinum sermonem conversus ab Henrico Maffacini*, Giunti Marzocco, Florence, 1963.

Gaddoni, Serafino, and Marrani, Adelmo, *Piancaldoli, memorie storico-artistiche*, Giampiero Pagnini Edit., Florence, reissue of the edition of 1932.

Lascialfari, Nello, *Il cardinal Antonio Bacci: note biografiche*, in *"Firenze e i suoi cardinali"*, edited by Gilberto Aranci, Pagnini Editore, Firenze, 2005.

Nardi, Carlo, *Latinità del cardinale Antonio Bacci: Contraddizioni e opportunità*, in *"Firenze e i suoi cardinali"*, edited by Gilberto Aranci, Pagnini Editore, Firenze, 2005.

Pagnini, Sara, *Profilo di Raffaello Caverni*, Pagnini-Martinelli Edit., Florence, 2001.

Piersanti, Carlo, and Fiorentini, Giorgio, *Piancaldoli: Un soggiorno distensivo nella Romagna Fiorentina*, Grafiche Liton, Casalfiumanese (Bologna)

Prantoni, Emilio, *Giugnola, il corpo e l'anima*, Bacchilega Edit., Imola, 2007.

Tagliaferri, Pier Carlo, and Tagliaferri, Luigi, *La banca del Mugello*, Lalli Edit., Poggibonsi (Siena) 1998.

Tagliaferri, Pier Carlo (editor), *Firenzuola e il suo territorio*, Lalli Edit., Poggibonsi (Siena), 1998.

ILLUSTRATIONS

```
IN HAC
RVSTICA DOMO
ANNO MDCCCLXXXV
PR. NON. SEPTEMBRES
ANTONIVS    BACCI
S. E. CARDINALIS
NATALEM DIEM VIDIT
LATINITATIS CVLTOR ET AMATOR IN PRIMIS
QVATTVOR ROMANORVM PONTIFICVM
LATINA VOX EXSTITIT
EORVMQVE PRAECEPTA NITIDE ORNAVIT
EX HVMILI POTENS FACTVS
NON NOMINE SED VIRTVTE CONFISUS
MODESTIAM VITAE VSQVE RETINVIT
VIR PIETATE INSIGNIS
QVOD INCONCVSSA FIDE CREDIDIT
HOC NVNC VIDET
```

Plaque erected at the entrance to the house in Giugnola where Cardinal Bacci was born

Translation of the inscription:

IN THIS RUSTIC HOUSE
IN THE YEAR 1885
ON SEPTEMBER 5
THERE FIRST SAW THE LIGHT OF DAY
ANTONIO BACCI
CARDINAL OF THE HOLY CHURCH
PREEMINENT STUDENT AND LOVER OF LATIN.
HE WAS THE LATIN VOICE OF FOUR ROMAN PONTIFFS
WHOSE TEACHINGS HE ADORNED WITH ELOQUENCE.
FROM HUMBLE BEGINNINGS HE ROSE TO BECOME GREAT
THROUGH HIS ABILITY NOT MERELY ON ACCOUNT OF HIS NAME.
HE REMAINED MODEST.
HE WAS A MAN NOTEWORTHY FOR HIS PIETY.
WHAT HE BELIEVED WITH A FIRM FAITH
THAT HE NOW SEES

Giugnola. The church dedicated to St. Dionysius

Panorama of Piancaldoli, from a souvenir postcard of 1928

Illustrations

Town center of Piancaldoli, from a postcard
bearing a cancellation from 1923

The picturesque hill of Saint Zenobius at Piancaldoli, near
where St. Zenobius, bishop of Florence, met St. Ambrose,
bishop of Milan. The fortress is connected with the famous
legend of the race between St. Zenobius and the devil.

The fortress of Caterina Sforza at Piancaldoli, from a postcard of 1942

The façade of the new parish church of Piancaldoli, from a postcard of 1927

The parish church of Casetta di Tiara, from
a photograph taken in 1915

The archiepiscopal seminary of Firenzuola, in a
photograph of 1900. The bust is that of the Archbishop
of Florence Antonio Martini, who was the founder.

Illustrations

Osservatorio (Padre Stopponi) - Interno Seminario Firenzuola

The archiepiscopal seminary of Firenzuola, the A. Stoppani tower, from a souvenir postcard of 1933

Via Giovanni Villani in Firenzuola. On the left one can see the porch of the Church of San Giovanni Battista. Also on the left is the town hall. On the right, along the road, are the buildings of the archiepiscopal seminary, nowadays the headquarters of the Banca di Mugello, from a souvenir postcard of 1937.

A photographic reproduction of the painting of Our Lady of Good Counsel, located in the apse of the chapel of the seminary of Firenzuola

Illustrations

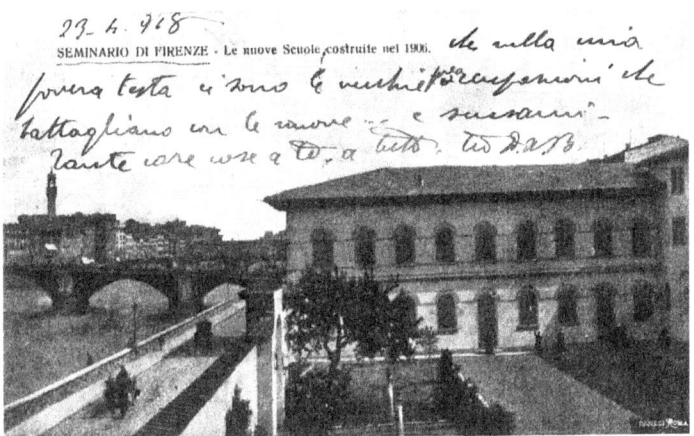

The new seat of the major seminary of Florence constructed in 1906. The postcard was sent in 1918; in those years Antonio Bacci was teacher and superior there.

Lecceto, near Malmantine, province of Florence, villa of the seminary of Florence. Here Cardinal Mistrangelo announced to Don Antonio Bacci his appointment to Rome, from a souvenir postcard dated 1946.

Mons. Antonio Bacci at Monte La Fineon during a trip with relatives and friends, at the end of the fifties of the preceding century.

Antonio Cardinal Bacci at dinner with the Poggi family in Firenzuola in 1960. From left to right his nephew Don Francesco Bacci, Don Anselmo Giovannardi, the holy pastor of San Pellegrino, the Cardinal, the daughter and wife of Signor Poggi, Don Ettore Mariotti, provost of Firenzuola, Don Giuliano Catani and Don Lionello Meucci, a Greek scholar of the highest rank.

Illustrations

Antonio Cardinal Bacci at Firenzuola in 1960 between the rector, Don Giuliano Catani, and the vice rector, Don Guelfo Falsini, on the terrace of the seminary

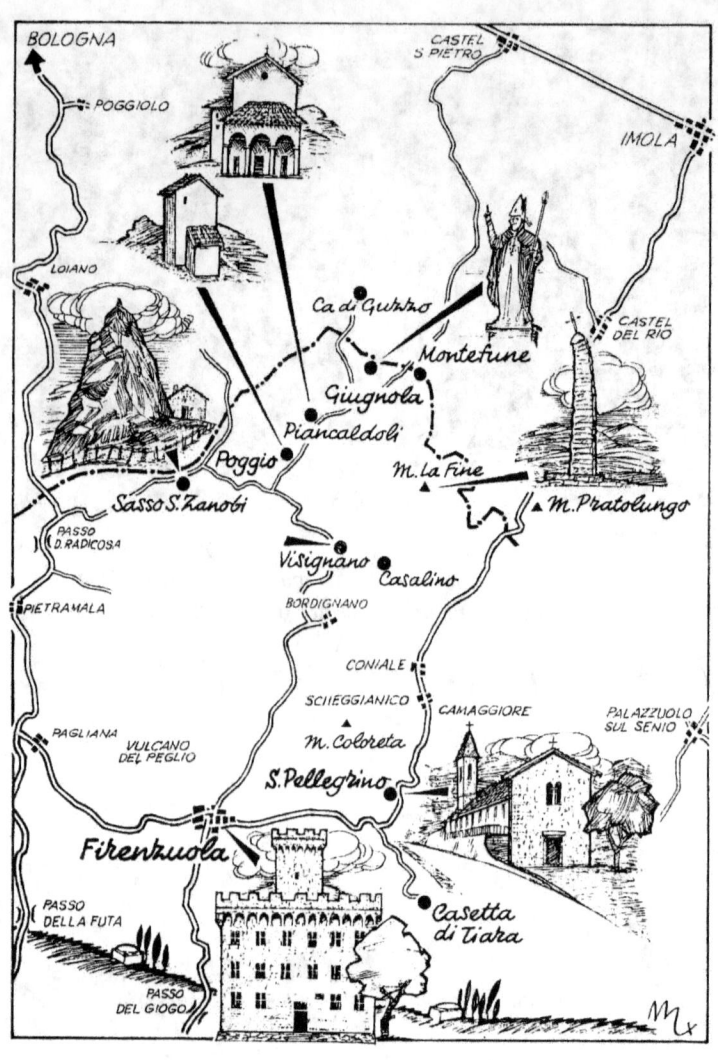

INDEX

ab Epistulis Summi Pontificis ad Principes, xii, 12, 18
Accademia dei Ravvivati, 24
Adeva, I., 20
Alla vergine di Lourdes (poem), 32
Addis Ababa, xl
Aloisi Masella, Benedetto Cardinal (1879–1970), xxvi
Ambrose, St. (*circa* 340–397), 65
Angelini, Filippo, lvii
Angelini, Gabriele, lv
Anthony of Padua, St. (1195–1231), 7, 57
Antibarbarus, xxxiv
Antonine Itinerary, xliii
Apuleius, 16
Arnobius (d. *circa* 330), xvi
Ars Italica (publishing house), 23, 61
Aubert, R., 17
Augustine, St. (354–430), xvi, xliii, lxiii, 15, 16, 17

Bacci, Agnese, 6
Bacci, Antonio Cardinal (1885–1971): appreciations of his books, xiv–xv; "Ciceronianism", 12–27; death and funeral, 3–8; on the ecumenical council, 3, 59–60; on Egger's *Lexicon nominum virorum et mulierum*, xxxvii–xxxviii; founding partner of a bank, liii–liv, lv–lvi; inscriptions, 49–55; introductions to his books, xiv, xviii–xxii, xxiii–xxvi; and *Latinitas*, xxvii–xxxi; and liturgical reform, 58–60; Memoirs, 34–38; poems, 23–33; translations, 42–46
Bacci, Bettina (d. 1896), 6
Bacci, Ettore (1887), 55
Bacci, Don Francesco, 72
Bacci, Marsilio, xxii

Bacci, Natalia, 54
Baddelino, O., 12
Bagnoli, Maestro Francesco (1876–1947), 6
Banca del Mugello, ix, liii, liv, lv, lvi, lxii, 70
Bastianensen, A. A. A., 19
Belletti, E., 51
Belli, Giuseppe Gioachino (1791–1863), 16
Bembo, Pietro (1470–1547), 14
Benelli, Don Giuseppe, 23
Benelli, Giovanni Cardinal (1921–1982), ix
Benham, Rev. William (1831–1910), lxi
Bethlehem, xl
Bianchi, A., xiv
Bloy, Léon (1846–1917), lix
Boggiani, Tommaso Pio Cardinal (1863–1942), xiii
Bonardi, Mons. Giulio, 6
Bonaccorsi, Salvi, 22
Breviary, Roman, lviii, 14, 57
Bruno, Pietro, xxii

Caelius Aurelianus (third, fourth, or fifth century AD), xvi
Caesar Augustus (63 BC–14 AD), 21
Calepino, Ambrogio (*circa* 1440–1510), 17
Calgacus (first century AD), 19
Campanini, G., 12
Candele che si spengono: Dalla parrocchia di montagna alla Curia Romana, 7, 56–57
Canons Regular of St. Augustine, lxiii
Capovilla, Loris Francesco Cardinal (1915–2016), lvii–lxiv
Carboni, G., 12
Carolingian Latin, 15

Casini, Nilo, 10, 11, 13
Casini, Stefano, 22, 24
Casini, Tito (1897–1987), x, lvii, lviii, lix, lxii, 40, 58, 59
Casetta di Tiara, 56, 68
Cassa Rurale di Prestiti e di Risparmio di Piancaldoli, 22
Castel del Rio, 1
Catani, Don Giuliano, 72, 73
Catechismus Romanus ad Parochos, 20
Catherine of Siena, St. (1347–1380), 59
Catullus (*circa* 84 BC–*circa* 54 BC), 22
Cento, Fernando Cardinal (1883–1973), xxvi
Church of the Ascension (Florence), 11
Church of San Giovanni Battista (Firenzuola), 70
Church of St. Dionysius (Giugnola), 64
Ciappi, Mario Luigi Cardinal (1909–1996), 7
Cicero (106 BC–43 BC), xvi, xvii, xviii, xix, xxi, xxxiv, xxxv, xxxvi, xlix, 9, 10, 11, 12, 13, 14, 15, 16, 17, 18, 19, 40
Ciceronianus sive de optimo dicendi genere, 14
Civiltà cattolica, 24
Clay, Cassius (boxer, 1942–2016), xxxii
Collegio Teologico Fiorentino, 5
Comparetti, Domenico, 11
Coniale, liii
Con il latino a servizio di quattro Papi, 34–38
Constitution on the Liturgy, 59, 60
Conte, Gian Biagio, 12
Cortesi, A., 18
Cortesi, Paolo (1471–1510), 14
Costa, Mons. Alberto, 41
Counter Reformation, 20
Cromwell, Oliver (1599–1658), xi
Curé d'Ars. *See* Vianney, Jean-Baptiste-Marie
Curia, Roman, xiv, 3, 56
Cyprian, St. (*circa* 200–258), 16

D'Ascenzo, Prof. Giuseppe (b. 1937), 41
De cardinalatu, 14
Del Ghio, Raffaello, 21
Dell'Acqua, Angelo Cardinal (1903–1972), xxxviii–xxxix
Della Rocca, Guglielmo (*circa* 1300–1354), 24
Del Ton, Giuseppe (1900–1997), xiii
De Lubac, Henri-Marie (1896–1991), lxiv
De Luca, Giuseppe, lviii–lix
De Marco, P., 18
Deutsch-lateinisches Wörterbuch, xli
De Vit, Vincenzo (1810–1892), xxxvii
Di Capua, Francesco (1879–1957), 18
Dionigi, Ivano (1948–), xxxii
Diomedes (*fl.* 375 AD), xvi
Dizionario di Italiano-Latino, 12
Döllinger, Ignaz von (1799–1890), l
Drigani, A., 19

Egger, Abbot Karl (1914–2003), xxxii, xxxiii, xxxiv, xxxviii, xxxix, xliv
Emilia, liv, 50, 51
Erasmus, Desiderius (1466–1536), 14
Esperanto, 60
Eugenianum, 11

Fairclough, H. R., xxv
Falsini, Don Guelfo, 73
Firenzuola, liii, lvii, lxii, 1, 5, 6, 11, 21, 22, 23, 24, 35, 48, 53, 56, 58, 68, 69, 70, 72, 73
Fliche, A., 17
Florence, ix, liii, lvii, 1, 4, 5, 6, 11, 12, 51, 53, 68, 71
Florence, University of, 11
Florit, Ermenegildo Cardinal (1901–1985), 4, 12
Forcellini, Egidio (1688–1768), xviii, 39
Foster, Reginald (1939–2020), xiii, xxxii, xlvi
Francis, Pope (1936– , reigned 2013–), l
Frazer, Joe (boxer, 1944–2011), xxxii
Fumaroli, M., 14

Index

Gaddoni, S., 51
Galeotti, Rev. Francesco, 52
Galli, Aurelio Cardinal (1866–1929), 1
Gambaro, A., 14
Gandiglio, A., xxi
George I, King of the United Kingdom (1660–1727, reigned 1714–1727), xi
Georges, Karl Ernst (1806–1895), 36
Gildersleeve, Basil Lanneau (1831–1924), xiii
Giovannardi, Don Anselmo, 72
Giugnola, 4, 7, 8, 22, 41, 63
Greek, xiii, xxii, xxxv, xxxvi, xl, xlii, xlv, xlvii, liii, 72
Guerriero, E., 17

Hagendahl, H., 16
Hammarskjöld, Dag (1905–1961), lxiii
Hebron, xl
Horace (65 BC–8 BC), xxv, 18

Imitation of Christ, lxi
Immè, Antonino (1901–1988), xxvii
Immè, Geneviève (1929–2012), xxvii
Imola, 22
Indo-European, xxxv
Inscriptiones Orationes Epistulae, 3, 12, 47–55
Istituto di Credito, lxii
Istituto di Studi Superiori, 11
Italian Bishops Conference, 60

Jerome, St. (*circa* 342–420), xvi, 10, 13, 16
Jerusalem, xlii
Jesuits, 14, 24
Jesus, lxiii, lxiv, 15
John XXIII (1881–1963, reigned 1958–1963), lv, lvii, lix, lxi, lxii, lxiii, 1, 2, 19, 34, 37, 38, 39
John Paul II (1920–2005, reigned 1978–2005), 40, 41
Jones, A. H. M., xliii
Julius Caesar (100 BC–44 BC), xvi

Kraft, Friedrich Karl (1786–1866), xli
Krebs, Johann Philipp (1771–1850), xxxiv

La battitura dei castagni (poem), 24, 29–31
La Calza e Castello, 11
Lactantius (*circa* 250–*circa* 325), xvi, 16
La farfalla azzurra (poem), 28
Lanzetti, R., 20
Lascialfari, Msgr. Nello (1923–2021), ix, x, 1–8
Late Latin, xvi, xxiii, xxv, xlv, li
Latinitas (journal), xxii, xxvi, xxvii, xxxi, xxxii, xxxiii, xxxix
Latinitas Foundation, xxxii, xxxix, xliv
Latin Letters Office of the Secretariat of State, xiii, xxxii
La tunica stracciata: lettera di un cattolico sulla "Riforma liturgica", 40, 58–60
Lecceto, 6, 34, 71
Leclerq, Fr. Jean, 15
Leo I, the Great (*circa* 400–461, reigned 440–461), 16
Leo XIII (1810–1903, reigned 1878–1903), xii, xviii, xlvi, 9
Lercaro, Giacomo Cardinal (1891–1976), lix–lxi
L'eroe (poem), 24–27
Lewis and Short Latin Dictionary, xxi
Lexicon eorum vocabulorum quae difficilius latine redduntur, xxxiii, xxxiv, xxxvii, xliv, lviii, 3, 12–13, 39. See also *Vocabolario italiano-latino delle parole moderne e difficili a tradurre*
Lexicon nominum locorum, xxxix–xliv
Lexicon nominum virorum et mulierum, xxxiii–xxxix
Lexicon recentis latinitatis, xliv–xlvi
Liceo Dante (Florence), 10
Liturgia horarum, 14

Livy (*circa* 61 BC–*circa* 15 AD), xvi
Loeb Classical Library, xxv
Lorini, Rev. Giulio, 5
Low Latin, xxiii, xxv, xl
Lucius Appuleius (fourth century BC), xvi
Luco di Mugello, liii
Lynch, Charles (1736–1786), xliv

Maffacini, Ettore, 41
Maglione, Luigi Cardinal (1877–1944), 1
Malmantine, 34, 71
Mancini, Lorenzo, 21
Marcellus Empiricus (fourth and fifth centuries AD), lvi
Mariotti, Don Ettore, 72
Maritain, Jacques (1882–1973), lix
Marrani, A., 51
Martina, G., 17
Martin, V., 17
Martini, Archbishop Antonio (1720–1809), 21, 52, 53, 68
Mediaeval Latin, xiv, xxviii, xl, 15, 16
Meditazioni per tutti i giorni dell' anno, x, 3
Menozzi, D., 18
Mercati, Giuseppe Cardinal (1866–1957), ix
Merino, M., 20
Meucci, Don Lionello (1885–1970), 72
Middle Ages, xxiii, xxxi, xxxiv, xxxvii, xliv, xlv, xlvii
Milan, xxxviii, 38, 65
Milton, John (1608–1674), xi, xlix
minutante, 1, 6, 35
Mistrangelo, Alfonso Maria Cardinal (1852–1930), 1, 6, 34, 35
Mohrmann, Christine (1903–1988), 16
Monte La Fineon, 72
Montini, Giovanni Battista. *See* Paul VI
Morcelli, Stefano Antonio (1737–1822), xviii, xxxvi
Moreschini, C., 10

Namaziano, Rutilio, 19
Nardi, Carlo (b. 1951), ix, x, 9–20
Norcia, xliii
Numidia, 19

Onomasticon, xxxvii
Oasi: Rime e ritmi giovanili, 6, 23
Oratio de eligendo pontifice, xii, 35, 37
Ovid (43 BC–*circa* 17 AD), xvi

Padovani, Don Giuseppe, 11
Palla, R., 10
Paoli, Ugo Enrico, 10, 13
Paratore, Ettore (1907–2000), xxxii
Parini, Giuseppe, lxii
Pascoli, Giovanni (1855–1912), 9, 11, 18
Pasquali, Giorgio, 11
Paul, Apostle (first century AD), lxiv
Paul VI (1897–1978, reigned 1963–1978), xiii, xiv, xv, xxvi, xxxviii, 38, 40, 48
Pavanetto, Anacleto (1931–2021), xxxii, xlvi
Pecci, Pope. *See* Leo XIII
Penitentiary, Apostolic, 3
Penna, A., 10
Perosi, Lorenzo (1872–1956), 22
Perin, Giuseppe (1845–1925), xxxvii
Perugia, xliii
Piancaldoli, liii, liv, lv, 22, 24, 48, 49, 65, 66, 67
Piancaldoli: Memorie storico-artistiche, 51
Pianezzola, Emilio, 12
Pico della Mirandola, Giovanni Francesco (1463–1494), 14, 36
Pifferi, Francesco, liv, 49, 51
Pighi, G. B., xix, xxi
Piovanelli, Silvano Cardinal (1924–2016), ix, x
Pisa, University of, 21
Pistelli, Ermenegildo, 11
Pius II (1405–1464, reigned 1458–1464), xii

Index

Pius XI (1857–1939, reigned 1922–1939), xxx, 1, 7, 34, 35, 39
Pius XII (1876–1958, reigned 1939–1958), xiii, xiv, xxx, xxxviii, 1, 2, 7, 34, 35, 36, 39, 48, 49
Pizzardo, Giuseppe Cardinal (1877–1970), xxvi
Poggi family, 72
Politian. *See* Poliziano, Angelo
Poliziano, Angelo (1454–1494), 14
Pompeii, 18
Prato, liv
Priscianus (*fl. circa* 500 AD), xvi, xx
Prometheus (journal), 11
Promm, K., 19
Prudentius (348–*circa* 413), xvi
Pugliese Carratelli, G., 11

Quintilian (*circa* 35–*circa* 100), xix, xx, xxi

Rahner, Karl (1904–1984), 19
Ranucci, Giuliano, 12
Ravagli, Rev. Antonio, 4
Ravasi, G., 16
Reformation, xi, 20
Ricciardi, R., 14
Rodriguez, P., 20
Roman Empire, xxi, xxvi, xxx, xl
Roman Republic, xxi
Rossano, P., 19
Ruffini, Paolo, ix, liii–liv

Sabbadini, A., 14
Sacred Congregation of the Council, 38
Sacred Congregation for Religious, 38
Sacred Congregation of Rites, 38
Sacred Congregation of Seminaries and Universities, 38
Sacrosanctum Concilium, 15, 20
Salutati, Coluccio (1331–1406), 18
Sanesi, Emilio, 11
San Francisco, xl

San Pellegrino, lvii, 72
Santa Cristina, 7
Santangelo, G., 14
Santerno (river), 24
Sant'Eugenio alle Belle Arti, 2
Savona, 34
Savonarola, Girolamo (1452–1498), 14
Schopenhauer, Arthur (1788–1860), xlvii– xlviii
Scilla, 19
Sebastiani, Nicola (1866 or 1867–1931), 1, 34
Second Vatican Council, lxiii, 3, 20, 37, 38, 40, 59
Secretary of Briefs to Princes, xii, xiii, xxxii, lv, lxiii, 1, 7, 35, 36, 38, 39, 41
Seneca (*circa* 4 BC–65 AD), 16
Sesto Fiorentino, liv
Sextus Aurelius Victor (*circa* 320–*circa* 390), xvi
Sforza, Caterina (1463–1509), 66
Sigismund, Holy Roman Emperor (1368–1437), xlviii
Smyrna, xliii
Stoppani, Antonio (1824–1891), 22, 69
Studio Teologico Fiorentino, 12
Suetonius (*circa* 69–*circa* 122), xxi

Tacitus (*circa* 56–*circa* 120), 16, 19
Tagliaferri, Don Carlino, 57
Tagliaferri, M., 12
Tagliaferri, Pier Carlo, ix, x, lv–lvi, 21–60
Tangier, xl
Tel Aviv, xl
Tertullian (*circa* 155–*circa* 240), xvi, 16
Thesaurus Linguae Latinae, xlv, xlvi, lxii
Tisserant, Eugène Cardinal (1884–1972), ix
Tommaseo, Niccolò (1802–1874), 21
Tondini, Amleto (1899–1969), xiii, xxii, xxxii

Tosi, R., 19
Trent, Council of, 20
Trentanove, Don, 5
Tuscany, ix, liv, 50, 51

Una Voce Federation, 59
Urban VIII (1568–1644, reigned 1623–1644), 14

Val di Pesa. 7
Varia latinitatis scripta, xiv, xv, 3, 12
Vatican II. *See* Second Vatican Council
Venturi, Luigi, 21
Vergil (70 BC–19 BC), 22
Vergine bella che di sol vestita, lv
via Giovanni Villani (Firenzuola), 70
Vianney, Jean-Baptiste-Marie (1786–1859), 57
Vitelli, Girolamo, 11

Vivens Homo (journal), 10, 11
Vocabolario della Lingua Italiana, 21
Vocabolario italiano-latino delle parole moderne e difficili a tradurre, xiii–xvi, 2, 36, 40, 41. *See also Lexicon eorum vocabulorum quae difficilius latine redduntur*
Volpini, Alessandro (1844–1903), xviii
Vox Latina, xxxiii

Walpole, Robert (1676–1745), xi
Wilamowitz-Möllendorff, Ulrich von, (1848–1931), 11
Wojtyła, Karol. *See* John Paul II

Zambarbieri, A., 17
Zannoni, Guglielmo, xxii
Zenobius, St. (337–417), 65

ABOUT THE TRANSLATOR

ANTHONY LO BELLO, A. B. (Kenyon College), M. S., M. Phil., Ph. D. (Yale University), is Professor of Mathematics at Allegheny College, Meadville, Pennsylvania. He is the author of four volumes published by Brill on the reception of Euclid's *Elements of Geometry* in the Middle Ages. His most recent books are *Origins of Mathematical Words: A Comprehensive Dictionary of Latin, Greek, and Arabic Roots* (Johns Hopkins University Press, Baltimore, 2013) and *Origins of Catholic Words: A Discursive Dictionary* (Catholic University of America Press, 2020). He was the authorized translator of *With Latin in the Service of the Popes: The Memoirs of Antonio Cardinal Bacci* (Arouca Press, 2020).

www.ingramcontent.com/pod-product-compliance
Lightning Source LLC
Chambersburg PA
CBHW071454070526
44578CB00001B/338